Essential

JAPANESE

Speak Japanese With Confidence

D0179190

TUTTLE Publishing

Tokyo │ Rutland, Vermont │ Singapore

The Tuttle Story: "Books to Span the East and West"

Most people are surprised to learn that the world's largest publisher of books on Asia had its humble beginnings in the tiny American state of Vermont. The company's founder, Charles E. Tuttle, belonged to a New England family steeped in publishing. And his first love was naturally books—especially old and rare editions.

Immediately after WW II, serving in Tokyo under General Douglas MacArthur, Tuttle was tasked with reviving the Japanese publishing industry. He later founded the Charles E. Tuttle Publishing Company, which still thrives today as one of the world's leading independent publishers.

Though a westerner, Tuttle was hugely instrumental in bringing a knowledge of Japan and Asia to a world hungry for information about the East. By the time of his death in 1993, Tuttle had published over 6,000 books on Asian culture, history and art—a legacy honored by the Japanese emperor with the "Order of the Sacred Treasure," the highest tribute Japan can bestow upon a non-Japanese.

With a backlist of 1,500 titles, Tuttle Publishing is more active today than at any time in its past—inspired by Charles Tuttle's core mission to publish fine books to span the East and West and provide a greater understanding of each.

Published by Tuttle Publishing, an imprint of Periplus Editions (HK) Ltd.

www.tuttlepublishing.com

Copyright © 2012 Periplus Editions

First Published in 1995 as Wat & Hoe Japans/@ Kosmos-Z&K Uitgevers in co-operation with Van Dale Lexicografie, Utrecht, The Netherlands

Library of Congress Control Number: 2012932262

ISBN 978-0-8048-4243-3
ISBN 978-4-8053-1236-0 (for sale in Japan only)

First edition
15 14 13 12   5 4 3 2 1   1203MP

Distributed by
North America, Latin America & Europe
Tuttle Publishing
364 Innovation Drive
North Clarendon, VT 05759-9436 U.S.A.
Tel: 1 (802) 773-8930; Fax: 1 (802) 773-6993
info@tuttlepublishing.com
www.tuttlepublishing.com

Japan
Tuttle Publishing
Yaekari Building, 3rd Floor, 5-4-12 Osaki
Shinagawa-ku, Tokyo 141 0032
Tel: (81) 3 5437-0171; Fax: (81) 3 5437-0755
sales@tuttle.co.jp   www.tuttle.co.jp

Asia Pacific
Berkeley Books Pte. Ltd.
61 Tai Seng Avenue #02-12,
Singapore 534167
Tel: (65) 6280-1330; Fax: (65) 6280-6290
inquiries@periplus.com.sg
www.periplus.com

Printed in Singapore

Contents

Introduction

● **Welcome to the Tuttle Essential Language series, covering all of the most popular world languages. These books are basic guides in communicating in the language. They're concise, accessible and easy to understand, and you'll find them indispensable on your trip abroad to get you where you want to go, pay the right prices and do everything you've been planning to do.**

Each guide is divided into 15 themed sections and starts with a pronunciation table which explains the phonetic pronunciation to all the words and sentences you'll need to know, and a basic grammar guide which will help you construct basic sentences in your chosen language. At the end of the book is an extensive English–Japanese word list.

Throughout the book you'll come across boxes with a 🔊 beside them. These are designed to help you if you can't understand what your listener is saying to you. Hand the book over to them and encourage them to point to the appropriate answer to the question you are asking.

Other boxes in the book—this time without the symbol—give alphabetical listings of themed words with their English translations beside them.

For extra clarity, we have put all phonetic pronunciations of the foreign language terms in italic.

This book covers all subjects you are likely to come across during the course of a visit, from reserving a room for the night to ordering food and drink at a restaurant and what to do if your car breaks down or you lose your traveler's checks and money. With over 2,000 commonly used words and essential sentences at your fingertips you can rest assured that you will be able to get by in all situations, so let *Essential Japanese* become your passport to learning to speak with confidence!

Pronunciation guide

Japanese is very easy to pronounce. It is made up of strings of syllables (**a**, **ka**, **ta**, etc.) which just join together following very simple rules of pronunciation (e.g. **anata** is *a-na-ta*). Unlike English, each syllable has mostly even stress and combinations of vowels (**e-i**, **a-i**, etc.) do not represent completely new sounds.

Vowels

Japanese has five vowels, pronounced either long or short. Distinguishing the length is very important as sometimes the meaning depends on the difference (e.g. **ojisan/ojiisan**, terms of address to a middle-aged man and an old man respectively). Note that a final **e** is always pronounced (e.g. **sake**, rice wine, is pronounced close to *sakay*).

a	like **a** in America	*a*	**asa**	*asa*	
ā	**ah** (as in the exclamation !)	*ah*	**mā**	*mah*	
e	**e** as in p**e**t or	*e*	**desu**	*des*	
	ay is in sw**ay**, but shorter	*ay*	**sake**	*sakay*	
ē	**eh** sounded long, like **ere** in there	*eh*	**eetone**	*eh-to-nay*	
i	like **i** in p**i**t, though slightly longer	*i*	**nichi**	*nichi*	
ī	**ee** as in k**ee**p	*ee*	**iie**	*ee-ye*	
o	**o** as in t**o**p	*o*	**yoru**	*yoru*	
ō	**ou** as in f**ou**r	*oh*	**kyō**	*kyoh*	
u	**u** as in p**u**t	*u*	**haru**	*haru*	
ū	**oo** as in c**oo**p	*oo*	**chūmon**	*choomon*	

Consonants

Most consonants are pronounced in a similar manner to English.

b	**b** as in **b**at	*b*	**bin**	*bin*
ch	**ch** as in **ch**ip	*ch*	**nichi**	*nichi*
d	**d** as in **d**ay	*d*	**dame**	*damay*

f	f as in **food**	*f*	**fuyu**	*fu-yu*
g	g as in **give**	*g*	**gogo**	*gogo*
h	h as in **hat**	*h*	**haru**	*haru*
j	j as in **jump**	*j*	**niji**	*niji*
k	k as in **king**	*k*	**koko**	*koko*
m	m as in **mat**	*m*	**totemo**	*totemo*
n	n as in **nut**; at the end of a word may be more like **ng**	*n*	**namae**	*nama-e*
		n(g)	**yen**	*yen (g)*
ng	ng as in **thing**	*ng*	**ringo**	*ring-o*
p	p as in **pat**	*p*	**posuto**	*pos-to*
r	Somewhere between English **r**, **l** and **d**. Never rolled **r**; more like **r** in car	*r*	**raigetsu**	*righ-gets*
s	s as in **start**	*s*	**semete**	*semetay*
sh	sh as in **ship**	*sh*	**shio**	*shi-o*
t	t as in **tip**	*t*	**dōshite**	*doh-shtay*
ts	ts as in **hits**	*ts*	**itsu**	*its*
w	w as in **watt**	*w*	**wakaru**	*wakaru*
y	y as in **yes**	*y*	**yoru**	*yoru*
z	z as in **zoo**	*z*	**mizu**	*mizu*

Note: when **i** and **u** follow **k**, **s**, **t**, **h**, **p** or come between two of them, they become very shortened and are often not heard at all (e.g. **desu** becomes *des* and **mimashita** becomes *mimashta*).

Vowel combinations

Basically, each vowel should be pronounced separately. The most common combinations are:

ai	igh as in **high**	*igh*	**hai**	*high*
ao	ow as in **now**	*ow*	**nao**	*now*
ei	ay as in **play**	*ay*	**rei**	*ray*
ue	weigh as in **weight**	*eigh*	**ue**	*weigh*

Basic grammar

1 Sentence construction

The greatest difference between Japanese and English sentences
is the position of the verb. In Japanese the verb always comes
last, giving the basic structure as subject–object–verb:

sensei wa *michi* o **oshiemashita** The teacher **showed** me the *way*

2 Parts of speech

Nouns Japanese nouns have no articles and no plural forms.
Zasshi (magazine), for example, could mean "a/the magazine,"
"magazines," or "the/some magazines." This might sound poten-
tially confusing to English speakers who expect the clear distinc-
tions that articles and plurals give. In actuality, though, very
little confusion exists, because Japanese has ways of indicating
number when it is necessary (see chapter 1).

Pronouns Japanese uses pronouns far less than English. They are
in fact often omitted when in the subject position. In English
we have to say "<u>who</u> went" in the sentence "I went to Kyoto
yesterday" if it is clear you are talking about yourself, in Japanese
you can merely say **kinoo Kyoto e ikimashita** (yesterday
to-Kyoto went). The most frequently used pronouns in Japanese
are **watashi** (I) and **anata** (you); 'he', 'she' and 'they' are far
more uncommon.

Adjectives Like in English, Japanese can use adjectives in two
ways, before the noun they describe (**mushiatsui** hi, a **humid**
day) or following it (kyoo wa **mushiatsui** desu, today is **humid**).
In grammatical terms, adjectives can in fact function as verbs,
and have tenses like verbs (see below).

Verbs The verb is probably the most important element in the
Japanese sentence, since it is quite possible for the sentence to
consist of a verb and nothing else:

tabemashita   (I, we, he, she, they, you, etc.) **ate**

Functions like tense, negation and level of politeness are shown by adding suffixes to the base form of the verb.

Whereas in English tense and agreement are probably the most important things about a verb, in Japanese the verb is the main way gradations of social status are marked. In the modern language there are three basic levels of politeness: the plain, or informal; the polite, or formal; and the honorific. If you look up a verb in the word list you will find it written in the base, or plain, form: for example, **taberu** (to eat) or **miru** (to see). This is the form used in informal conversation, so, for example, you might say to a friend "**ashita ii restoran ni iku**" (tomorrow I— to a good restaurant—am going). However, when you talk to people you have only just met or to someone senior to you, you must use the polite form, for example, "**ashita ii restoran ni ikimasu.**" The **-masu** ending always indicates the polite level. The honorific level is used when someone wishes to show extreme politeness, either because of their own humble position (a shop assistant to a customer, for example) or because of the exalted nature of the person he or she is speaking with (like a company president). Honorific language is very complicated and even Japanese people find it difficult. In this phrasebook, the informal level has been used in close personal situations, the polite in general conversation, and the honorific only when showing how someone in a service situation might address you.

In comparison to English the form of Japanese tenses is simple. The future tense has the same form as the present, so that **tabemasu** could mean "I eat" or "I will eat." The past is shown by adding the suffix **ta**: tabemashita (I ate), mimashita (I saw). The only other form used for tense is the continuative, made using the suffix **te**: tabete imasu (I am eating); **tabete imashita** (I was eating). English speakers may find the lack of a perfect tense (I have done—) confusing, but Japanese employs other, non-verb forms, to express this.

The negative is made by adding the suffix **nai** to the plain form of the verb, for example, **tabenai** (I do not eat), or the suffix **n** to the polite **masu** ending, for example, **tabemasen** (I do not eat).

3 Particles

Japanese is very different from English in that the relationships between the various parts of speech are shown by the use of particles. English uses word order to indicate meaning: "the dog bit the man" and "the man bit the dog" are different entirely because of the order in which the words come in a sentence. In Japanese the meaning is not dependent on word order but on particles; the doer of the action (subject) is shown by the particle **ga** and receiver of the action (object) is shown by the particle **o**:

inu ga hito o kanda (literally, the dog—the man—bit: the dog bit the man)

hito ga inu o kanda (literally, the man—the dog—bit: the man bit the dog)

Japanese has another particle, **wa**, which often marks the subject as well. This has the function of pointing out a particular word and making it stand out from the rest of the sentence as the topic.

kono seki wa aite imasu ka? (as for this seat, is it free: is this seat free?)

koko ni wa nani ka omoshiroi no ga arimasu ka? (as for in this place, is there anything interesting here: is there anything interesting here?)

The above examples also show the use of the question-making particle **ka**.

Another important particle is **no**, used principally to join nouns together, so functioning like the English possessive.

watashi no namae (literally, the name of me; my name)

igirusu no shimbun (literally a newspaper of England; an English newspaper)

Other particles act like English prepositions: **ni** (at, in, on, to), **e** (to a place), **de** (at, with), **kara** (from), **made** (to, until), and **yori** (from).

4 Some useful grammatical forms

The phrase book has shown you how to say things as you need

them in different situations. Let us bring together some useful forms that might help you to make new sentences, using words from the wordlist.

Please do something A general imperative is the **-te kudasai** *(-te kuda-sigh)* ending added to a verb:

taberu (eat)	**tabete kudasai**	please eat
miseru (show)	**misete kudasai**	please show me
kuru (come)	**kite kudasai**	please come
kaku (write)	**kaite kudasai**	please write

You can negate this with the phrase **naide kudasai** *(nigh-de kuda-sigh)*:

taberu	**tabenaide kudasai**	please don't eat
miseru	**misenaide kudasai**	please don't show me
kuru	**konaide kudasai**	please don't come
kaku	**kakanaide kudasai**	please don't write

Have to do The most usual way of showing necessity is **-nakereba narimasen**:

iku	**ikanakereba narimasen**	I have to go
suru	**shinakereba narimasen**	I have to do
miru	**minakereba narimasen**	I have to see

Want You can show that you want to do something by adding **-tai n(o) desu** *(-tigh n(o) des)* to the verb:

iku	**ikitai n desu**	I want to go
yomu	**yomitai n desu**	I want to read
miru	**mitai n desu**	I want to see

Please When you want someone to do something for you, say **onegai shimasu**, literally "I beg of you". This is a useful phrase that can be used in a variety of ways. If someone offers to do something for you, you can use it to accept:

biiru wa doo desu ka	would you like some beer?
Onegai shimasu	yes, please

If you want an item in a shop, say what it is with '**onegai shimasu**':

hon onegai shimasu	a book, please
pan onegai shimasu	bread, please

Useful verbs Two of the most useful verbs are **desu** *(des)*, equivalent of 'is/are' and **arimasu** *(arimas)*, 'there is/are':

watashi wa Igirisujin **desu**	I **am** English
aita heya wa **arimasu ka**	**are there** any vacancies?

5 A final tip

The Japanese language is full of loan words, most of them from English. They are used to name things, and so are almost always nouns. If you get stuck for a word, try pronouncing the English word slowly in a Japanese way. For example, if you pronounce 'bus station' syllable by syllable, *ba-su su-tay-shon*, this will turn out to be a perfectly understandable Japanese word.

The Japanese writing system

Written Japanese combines three different scripts, *hiragana*, *katakana* and *kanji*. Hiragana consists of 46 syllabic characters and is used to write the grammatical elements of the Japanese sentence, like particles and verb endings. Katakana also has 46 characters, and is used to write foreign words. The meaningful component of the sentence is written with *kanji* (Chinese characters), that is, nouns, adjectives, some adverbs and the base form of verbs.

Igirisu no **hon** o **kai**mashita	I bought an English book

Igirisu will be written in katakana, being a foreign word, **hon** and **ka** in Chinese characters, and the remaining syllables in hiragana.

Place names on station notice boards will almost always be written in *kanji*, but the pronunciation in *hiragana* is also given beneath. In the large cities, the pronunciation in the latin alphabet (*romaji*, 'Roman letters') will also appear. The *kanji* give the meaning to the word. For example, To-kyo means 'eastern capital', O-saka means 'great slope', Hane-da means 'field of wings' and Roppon-gi means 'six trees.'

1 The Basics

1. The Basics

 1.1 **Personal details**

In Japan the family name comes first and the given name next. Titles come after the name. The title -*san* can be attached either to the surname or the given name, and is used for both males and females, being the equivalent of Mr. Mrs and Miss. Small children are addressed by their given name plus -*chan*, and boys by either their given name (among friends) or their surname (at school, for example) plus -*kun*. Superiors may also address subordinates in companies by their surname plus -*kun*. Anyone regarded as an intellectual is called **sensei** (*sen-say*, 'teacher').

your name	*onama-e* お名前
my name	*nama-e* 名前
surname	*myohji/say* 名字（苗字）／姓
given name(s)	*nama-e* 名前
address	*joo-sho* 住所
postal/zip code	*yoobin bango* 郵便番号
sex (male/female)	*say (dan/jo)* 性（男／女）
nationality	*koku-seki* 国籍
date of birth	*say-nen-gappi* 生年月日
place of birth	*shushoh-chi* 出生地

occupation	*shoku-gyoh* 職業
married/single/divorced	*ki-kon/mi-kon/ri-kon* 既婚／未婚／離婚
(number of) children	*ko-domo (no kazu)* 子供（の数）
passport/identity card/ driving license number	*pasu-pohto (ryo-ken)/mibun shoh-may- sho/unten men-kyo-sho no bango* パスポート（旅券）／身分証明書／ 運転免許書の番号

1.2 Today or tomorrow?

What day is it today?	*Kyoh-wa nan-yohbi des-ka* 今日は何曜日ですか。
Today's Monday	*Kyoh-wa gets-yohbi des* 今日は月曜日です。
– Tuesday	*Kyoh-wa ka-yohbi des* 今日は火曜日です。
– Wednesday	*Kyoh-wa swee-yohbi des* 今日は水曜日です。
– Thursday	*Kyoh-wa moku-yohbi des* 今日は木曜日です。
– Friday	*Kyoh-wa kin-yohbi des* 今日は金曜日です。
– Saturday	*Kyoh-wa do-yohbi des* 今日は土曜日です。
– Sunday	*Kyoh-wa nichi-yohbi des* 今日は日曜日です。
What's the date today?	*Kyoh-wa nan-gatsu nan-nichi des-ka* 今日は何月何日ですか。
in January	*ichi-gatsu-ni* 一月に

since February	*ni-gatsu-kara* 二月から
in spring	*haru-ni* 春に
in summer	*natsu-ni* 夏に
in autumn	*aki-ni* 秋に
in winter	*fuyu-ni* 冬に
2012	*ni-sen joo-ni nen* 2012年
the twentieth century	*nijoo-say-ki* 20世紀
the twenty-first century	*nijoo-is-say-ki* 21世紀
What's the date today?	*Kyoh-wa nan-nichi des-ka* 今日は何日ですか。
Today's the 24th	*Kyoh-wa nijoo-yokka des* 今日は24日です。
Monday 3 November 2012	*Ni-sen joo-ni nen joo-ichi-gatsu* *mikka gets-yohbi* 2012年11月3日 月曜日。
in the morning	*asa-ni* 朝に
in the afternoon	*gogo-ni* 午後に
in the evening	*yoogata-ni* 夕方に
at night	*yoru-ni* 夜に
this morning	*kesa* 今朝
this afternoon	*kyoh no gogo* 今日の午後

this evening	*kyoh no yoogata* 今日の夕方
tonight	*kom-ban* 今晩
last night	*saku-ban* 昨晩
this week	*kon-shoo* 今週
next month	*righ-gets* 来月
last year	*kyo-nen* 去年
next...	*tsugi-no* 次の
in...days/weeks/months/ years	*...nichi/shookan/ka-getsu/nenkan-ni* …日／週間／か月／年間に
...weeks ago	*...shookan ma-e-ni* …週間前に
day off	*kyoo-jitsu* 休日

 ## 1.3 **What time is it?**

What time is it now?	*Ima nanji des-ka* 今何時ですか。
It's nine o'clock	*(gozen) ku-ji des* （午前）9時です。
– five past ten	*(gozen) joo-ji go-fun...* （午前）10時5分…
– a quarter past eleven	*(gozen) joo-ichi-ji joo-go-fun...* （午前）11時15分…
– twenty past twelve	*(gogo) joo-ni-ji ni-juppun...* （午後）12時20分…

– half past one	*(gogo) ichi-ji han...* （午後）1時半…
– twenty-five to three	*(gogo) ni-ji san-joo-go-fun...* （午後）2時35分…
– a quarter to four	*(gogo) san-ji yon-joo-go-fun...* （午後）3時45分…
– ten to five	*(gogo) yo-ji go-juppun...* （午後）4時50分…
– twelve noon	*joo-ni-ji/shoh-go...* 12時／正午…
– midnight	*yo-naka no joo-ni-ji...* 夜中の12時…
half an hour	*san-juppun-kan* 三十分間
What time?	*Nanji* 何時？
What time can I come by?	*Nanji-ni kureba ee des-ka* 何時に来れば いいですか。
At...	*... ni* …に
After...	*... sugi-ni* …過ぎに
Before...	*... ma-e-ni* …前に
Between...and...	*... to ... no ai-da-ni...* …と…の間に
From...to...	*... kara ... maday* …から…まで
In...minutes	*... fun go-ni* …分後に
– an hour	*... ichi-jikan go-ni* 1時間後に
– ...hours	*... jikan go-ni* …時間後に

– a quarter of an hour	*joo-go-fun go-ni* 15分後に
– three quarters of an hour	*yon-joo-go-fun go-ni* 45分後に
early/late	*haya-sugi-mas/oso-sugi-mas* 早過ぎます／遅過ぎます。
on time	*mani-attay/... ni mani-a-imas* 間に合って／…に間に合います。
I will be a little bit late	*Sukoshi okure mas* 少し遅れます。
I am sorry I am late	*Okurete sumi masen* 遅れてすみません。

1.4 One, two, three...

Numbers are rarely used on their own, but join with 'counters'.
The counter can be joined after any of the numbers in the list
below. For example, the counter for books is satsu, so that 'one
book' is/**is-satsu**/, 'two books' is/**ni-satsu**/, etc.

Some of the most common counters are:

時 *ji* (hour): *ichi-ji* (1 o'clock), *ni-ji* (2 o'clock)

時間 *jikan* (hours): *ichi-jikan* (1 hour), *ni-jikan* (two hours)

枚 *mai* (used for flat objects like sheets of paper): *ichi-migh,
ni-migh*, etc.

円 *yen* (the Japanese currency): *hyaku-en* (100 yen), *sen(g)-
en* (1000 yen)

台 *dai* (for machines like cars and bikes): *ichi-digh, ni-digh*, etc.

杯 *hai* (cups): *koh-hee ni-high* (two cups of coffee), *o-cha go-
high* (five cups of tea)

本 *hon* (for cylindrical objects, like chopsticks, cigarettes,
etc.): *ip-pon, ni-hon, sam-bon*

人 *nin* (people): *san-nin* (three people), *roku-nin* (six people).
The words for one and two people are different: *hi-to-ri* (one
person) and *fu-ta-ri* (two people).

However you can avoid using counters for the numbers one to ten by employing the alternative Japanese numbering system. They are shown in brackets in the list. For example, *hambahga mits kuda-sigh* is "Two hamburgers, please."

0	*ray/zero*
1	*ichi (hi-tots)*
2	*ni (fu-tats)*
3	*san (mits)*
4	*shi/yon (yots)*
5	*go (i-tsuts)*
6	*roku (muts)*
7	*shichi/nana (na-nats)*
8	*hachi (yats)*
9	*ku/kyoo (koko-nots)*
10	*joo/ju (toh)*
11	*joo-ichi*
12	*joo-ni*
13	*joo-san*
14	*joo-shi*
15	*joo-go*
16	*joo-roku*
17	*joo-shichi*
18	*joo-hachi*
19	*joo-ku*
20	*ni-joo*
21	*ni-joo-ichi*
22	*ni-joo-ni*
30	*san-joo*
31	*san-joo-ichi*
32	*san-joo-ni*
40	*yon-joo*
50	*go-joo*
60	*roku-joo*
70	*nana-joo*
80	*hachi-joo*
90	*kyoo-joo*

100	*hyaku*
101	*hyaku ichi*
110	*hyaku joo*
120	*hyaku ni-joo*
200	*ni-hyaku*
300	*sam-byaku*
400	*yon-hyaku*
500	*go-hyaku*
600	*rop-pyaku*
700	*nana-hyaku*
800	*hap-pyaku*
900	*kyoo-hyaku*
1000	*sen/issen*
1100	*sen hyaku*
2000	*ni-sen*
3000	*san-zen*
8000	*has-sen*
10,000	*ichi-man*
20,000	*ni-man*
100,000	*joo-man*
a million	*hyaku-man*
one hundred million	*oku*
1st	*dai-ichi* 第一
2nd	*dai-ni* 第二
3rd	*dai-san* 第三
once	*ichi-bigh* 一倍
twice	*ni-bigh* 二倍
triple	*sam-bigh* 三倍
half	*ham-bun* 半分

a quarter	*yon-bun no ichi* 四分の一
a third	*sam-bun no ichi* 三分の一
a couple, a few, some	*iku-tsu ka no/ni, san* いくつかの／二、三
2 + 4 = 6	*ni tas yon wa roku* 2たす4は6
4 − 2 = 2	*yon hiku ni wa ni* 4ひく2は2
2 x 4 = 8	*ni kakeru yon wa hachi* 2かける4は8
4 ÷ 2 = 2	*yon waru ni wa ni* 4割る2は2
odd/even	*goo-soo no/ ki-soo no* 偶数の／奇数の
total	*zem-bu (de)* 全部（で）
6 x 9	*Nagasa wa kyoo meh-toru haba wa roku meh-toru des* 長さは9メートル幅は6メートルです。

1.5 The weather

Is the weather going to be good/bad?	*Ee/waru-i tenki ni narimas-ka?* いい／悪い天気になりますか。
Is it going to get colder/hotter?	*Samuku/atsuku narimas-ka?* 寒く／暑くなりますか。
What temperature is it going to be?	*Ondo wa nandou gura-i deshoka?* 気温は何度ぐらいでしょうか。
Is it going to rain?	*Amay ni narimas-ka?* 雨になりますか。
Is there going to be a storm?	*Arashi ni narimas-ka?* 嵐になりますか。

Is it going to snow? *Yuki ni narimas-ka?*
雪になりますか。

Is it going to freeze? *Kohri ga harimas-ka?*
氷が張りますか。

Nice breeze *Ee kaze des-ne*
いい風ですね。

Is there going to be a *Righ-u ni narimas-ka?*
thunderstorm? 雷雨になりますか。

Is it going to be foggy? *Kiri ga tachimas-ka?*
霧が立ちますか。

The weather's changing *Tenki-ga kuzuremas*
天気がくずれます。

It's cooling down *Suzushiku narimas.*
涼しくなります。

What's the weather *Kyoh/ashta no tenkl yo-hoh wa doh*
going to be like today/ *des-ka?*
tomorrow? 今日／明日の天気予報はどうですか。

薄ら寒い chilly	嵐 stormy	酷暑 heat wave	はやて squalls
快晴 clear	暑い hot	日当りのよい sunny	雪 snow
曇 cloudy	台風 typhoon	雷雨 thunderstorm	ひょう hail
寒い cold	穏やか mild	雨天 wet	暖かい warm
湿っぽい damp	蒸し暑い muggy	風 wind	霧 fog
どんよりした overcast	霧雨 drizzle	風のある windy	霜 frost
梅雨 rainy season	いい天気 fine	猛暑 scorching hot	霰 sleet
(氷点下) …度 ...degrees (above/ below zero)	にわか雨 shower	かすかな／強い風 light/moderate/ strong wind	雨 rain

1.6 **Here, there...**

See also 5.1 Asking directions

here/there	*koko/soko/a-soko* ここ…そこ…あそこ
somewhere	*doko-ka* どこか
nowhere	*doko ni mo...nai* どこにも…ない
everywhere	*doko ni demo* どこにでも
far away/nearby	*toh-i/chi-kigh* 遠い…近い
right/left	*migi no hoh ni/hidari no hoh ni* 右の方に…左の方に
to the right/left of	*... no migi ni/... no hidari ni* …の右に／…の左に
straight ahead	*mas-sugu* 真っ直ぐ
via	*... kay-yu de* …経由で
in	*... no naka ni* …の中に
on	*... no u-e ni* …の上に
under	*... no shta ni* …の下に
against	*... ni tigh-shtay* …に対して
opposite	*... no mukoh-gawa ni* …の向こう側に
next to	*... no tonari ni* …の隣に

near	... *no soba ni* …の側に
in front of	... *no ma-e ni* …の前に
in the center	... *no man-naka ni* …の真ん中に
forward	*ma-e ay* 前へ
down	*shta ay* 下へ
up	*u-e ay* 上へ
inside	*naka ay* 中へ
outside	*soto ay* 外へ
behind	*ushiro ay* 後へ
at the front	*ma-e ni* 前に
at the back	*ushiro ni* 後に
in the north	*kita no hoh ni* 北の方に
to the south	*minami no hoh ni* 南の方へ
from the west	*nishi no hoh kara* 西の方から
from the east	*hi-gashi no hoh kara* 東の方から

1.7 What does that sign say?

緊急ブレーキ／
非常ブレーキ
Emergency brake

緊急出口／非常口
Emergency exit

通行禁止
No thoroughfare

手をふれないで
ください。
Please do not touch

ペンキ塗りたて
Wet paint

芝生に入らないで
下さい。
Keep off the grass

起こさないで
ください。
Do not disturb

観光案内所
Tourist information

トイレ／お手洗い／
便所（女性／男性）
Toilets/Gents/
  Gentlemen/Ladies

携帯電話の通話は
ご遠慮下さい。
Do not use cell
  phone here

マナーモードに設定
して下さい。
Put cell phone on
  silence mode

受付け
Reception

禁煙
No smoking

喫煙
Smoking

押／引
Push/pull

故障中
Out of order

予約済
Reserved

売出し
Sale/
  clearance

売り物
For sale

案内
Information

エスカレー
ター
Escalator

エレベー
ター
Elevator

清掃中
Cleaning

避難階段
Fire escape

私有地
Private
  (property)

待合室
Waiting room

停留所／バス停
Bus stop

停車場／
  タクシー乗り場
Taxi stand

郵便箱／ポスト
Post box

猛犬注意
Beware of the
  dog

火気厳禁
No open fires

高圧注意
High voltage

足下注意
Watch your step

頭上注意
"Low clearance"

ペット禁止
No pets allowed

営業時間
Opening hours

警察署
Police station

撮影禁止
No photographs

お会計／お支払
Pay here

危険
Danger

注意
Warning

応急手当
First aid

〒
Mail

入口
Entrance

出口
Exit

銀行
Bank

窓口
Counter

切符
Tickets

階
...floor

営業中
Open

準備中
Closed

満員
Full

階段
Stairs

立入禁止
No entry

The Basics

1

1.8 Legal holidays

New Year's Day (January 1)	*gan-jitsu*
Coming of Age Day (2nd Monday of January)	*sayjin-no-hi*
National Foundation Day (February 11)	*ken-koku ki-nen-bi*
Vernal Equinox Day (March 21)	*shun-bun-no-hi*
Showa Day (April 29)	*midori-no-hi*
Constitution Day (May 3)	*kempoh ki-nen-bi*
Public Holiday (May 4)	*kokumin-no-kyoo-jitsu*
Children's Day (May 5)	*kodomo-no-hi*
Marine Day (3rd Monday of July)	*umi-no-hi*
Respect for the Aged Day (3rd Monday of September)	*kayroh-no-hi*
Autumnal Equinox Day (September 23)	*shoo-bun-no-hi*
Health-Sports Day (2nd Monday of October)	*tigh-iku-no-hi*
Culture Day (November 3)	*bunka-no-hi*
Thanksgiving Day (November 23)	*kinroh-kansha-no-hi*
Emperor's Birthday (December 23)	*tennoh tanjoh-bi*

Though officially only January 1 is a public holiday during the New Year period, most banks and businesses remain shut until at least January 3. The period between April 29 and May 5 is known as Golden Week.

The Obon festival, when families return to ancestral homes to venerate the returning spirits of their ancestors, is held in country districts around mid July and in Tokyo in mid August. It should also be noted that Christmas Day is a normal business day.

2 Meet and Greet

2. Meet and Greet

The use of courtesies is considered important in Japan. When someone does something for you, a simple *dohmo sumimasen* (thank you for your trouble) is greatly appreciated. On meeting, the Japanese greet each other with a bow from the waist, of varying depth. Non-Japanese need not do so, though this is a custom which people find themselves following almost unconsciously after a short time. Men in particular may greet a European with a handshake. It is of utmost importance that shoes are taken off when entering private homes. There is a greater tolerance of proximity in Japan than in the U.S.; in trains, elevators and other crowded public places, physical contact is unavoidable. It is polite, however, to maintain a kind of mental privacy. Impatience is rarely shown in public, while displays of anger cause embarrassment and are rarely effective.

2.1 Greetings

Good morning	*O-high-yoh (goza-i-masu)* おはよう（ございます）。
Hello	*Kon-nichi wa* こんにちは。
Good evening	*Kom-ban wa* 今晩は。
Good afternoon	*Kon-nichi wa* 今日は。
How are you?	*O-genki des-ka* お元気ですか。
Fine, thank you, and you?	*High, genki des. anata wa* はい、元気です。あなたは？
Very well	*O-kagay-sama day* おかげさまで。
Not too bad	*Mah mah des* まあまあです。

I'd better be going	*Jah, shi-tsu-ray shimas* じゃあ、失礼します。

I have to be going.
  Someone's waiting
  for me
	Shto-o matasetay imas no day,
	koray-de shi-tsu-ray itashimas
	人を待たせていますので、
	これで失礼いたします。

Good bye	*Sayoh-nara* さよなら。
See you soon	*Mata ato-day* またあとで。
Good night	*Oyasumi nasa-i* お休みなさい。
Good luck	*Gambattay kuda-sigh* がんばって下さい。
Have fun	*Tano-shinday kuda-sigh* 楽しんで下さい。
Have a nice vacation	*Tanoshee kyookay-o* 楽しい休暇を。
Have a good trip	*Tanoshee ryokoh-o* 楽しい旅行を。
Thank you, you too	*Dohmo arigatoh, anata-mo* どうもありがとう。あなたも。
Say hello to...for me	*... ni yoroshku* …によろしく。

2.2 Asking a question

Who?	*Daray* 誰？
Who's that?	*Daray des-ka* 誰ですか。
What?	*Nani* 何？

What's there to see here?	*Kono chikaku day nani-ka omoshiroi koto-ga arimas-ka* この近くで何か面白いことがありますか。
What kind of hotel is that?	*Donna hoteru des-kadonna hoteru des-ka* どんなホテルですか。
Where?	*Doko* どこ？
Where's the bathroom?	*Toiray-wa doko-ni arimas-ka* トイレはどこにありますか。
Where are you going?	*Dochira-ni ikaremas-ka* どちらに行かれますか。
Where are you from?	*Doko-kara kimashta-ka* どこから来ましたか。
How?	*Doh* どう？
How far is that?	*Dono kurigh toh-i des-ka* どのくらい遠いですか。
How long does that take?	*Nan-jikan kakarimas-ka* 何時間かかりますか。
How long is the trip?	*Ryokoh-wa dono kurigh kakarimas-ka* 旅行はどのくらいかかりますか。
How much?	*Ikura des-ka* いくらですか。
How many?	*Ikutsu des-ka* いくつですか。
How much is this?	*Koray-wa ikura des-ka* これはいくらですか。
Which....?	*Dono...* どの…？
Which?	*Doray...* どれ？
Which glass is mine?	*Dono koppu-ga watashi-no des-ka* どのコップが私のですか。

When?	*Itsu* いつ？
When are you leaving?	*Itsu demas-ka* いつ出ますか。
Why?	*Dohshtay/nazay* どうして／なぜ
Could you help me, please?	*Tetsudattay kudasa-i-masen-ka* 手伝って下さいませんか。
Could you point that out to me?	*Oshietay kudasa-i-masen-ka* 教えて下さいませんか。
Could you come with me, please?	*Tsuretay ittay kudasa-i-masen-ka* 連れていって下さいませんか。
Could you reserve some tickets for me, please?	*Yoyaku shitay itadakemas-ka* 予約していただけますか。
Do you know...?	*... (o) shtte imas-ka* …（を）知っていますか。
Do you know another hotel, please?	*Hoka-no hoteru-o shohkaigh shtay kuda-sigh* 他のホテルを紹介して下さい。
Do you have a...?	*... (ga) arimas-ka* …（が）ありますか。
Do you have a vegetarian dish, please?	*Bejitarian-ryohri-wa arimas-ka* ベジタリアン料理はありますか。
I'd like...	*... onega-i-shimas* …お願いします。
I'd like a kilo of apples, please	*Ringo-o ikkiro kuda-sigh* リンゴを一キロ下さい。
Can I take this?	*Kore-o mottay ittay-mo ee des-ka* これを持って行ってもいいですか。
Can I smoke here?	*Tabako-o suttay-mo ee des-ka* タバコを吸ってもいいですか。
Could I ask you something?	*Sumimasen-nga* すみませんが

2.3 How to reply

Yes, of course	*High, mochiron* はい、もちろん。
No, I'm sorry	*Ee-ye, sumimasen* いいえ、すみません。
Yes, what can I do for you?	*High, dohzo* はい、どうぞ。
Just a moment, please	*Chotto mattay kudasa-i* ちょっと待って下さい。
No, I don't have time now	*Sumimasen-nga, jikan-nga arimasen* すみませんが、時間がありません。
No, that's impossible	*Fukanoh des* 不可能です。
I think so	*Soh omo-imas* そう思います。
No, no one	*Dare-mo imasen* 誰もいません。
No, nothing	*Nan demo arimasen* 何でもありません。
It's okay	*Die-joh-bu des* 大丈夫です。
That's right	*Soray-day kekkoh des* それで結構です。
That's different	*Chiga i masu* 違います。
I agree	*Sansay des* 賛成です。
I don't agree	*Sansay dekimasen* 賛成出来ません。
All right	*Ee des* いいです。
Okay	*Ee des-yo* いいですよ

| Perhaps | *Tabun*
多分 |
| I don't know | *Wakarimasen/shirimasen*
わかりません／知りません |

2.4 Thank you

Thank you	*(dohmo) arigatoh* (どうも) ありがとう。
You're welcome	*Doh itashi-mashtay* どういたしまして。
Thank you very much	*Dohmo arigatoh goza-i-mas* どうもありがとうございます。
Very kind of you	*Go-shinsetsu-ni* ご親切に！
I enjoyed it very much	*Hontoh-ni tanoshikatta des* 本当に楽しかったです。
Thank you for your trouble	*Dohmo arigatoh goza-i-mashta* どうもありがとうございました
You shouldn't have	*Sumimasen deshta* すみませんでした。
That's all right	*Doh itashimashtay* どういたしまして。

2.5 I'm sorry

Excuse me	*Sumimasen* すみません
I'm sorry, I didn't know...	*... Shiranakatta no-day, mohshi-wakay-arimasen* …知らなかったので、申し訳ありません。
I do apologize	*Sumimasen deshta* すみませんでした。

I'm sorry	*Mohshi-wakay-arimasen* 申し訳ありません。
I didn't do it on purpose, it was an accident	*Waza-to yatta wakay de-wa-nai* *no-day, oyurushi-kuda-sigh* わざとやったわけではないので、 お許し下さい。
That's all right	*Ee des-yo* いいですよ
Never mind	*Mah mah* まあまあ
It could've happened to anyone	*Soray-wa daray-ni demo okori-eru* *koto des* それは誰にでも起こりえることです。

2.6 What do you think?

Which do you prefer?	*Dochira-ga o-ski des-ka* どちらがお好きですか。
What do you think?	*Doh omoimas-ka* どう思いますか。
Don't you like dancing?	*Odoru no-ga ki-righ es-ka* 踊るのが嫌いですか。
I don't mind	*Nandemo ee des* 何でもいいです。
Well done!	*Yokatta* よかった。
Not bad!	*Waruku-nai des-ne* 悪くないですね！
Great!	*Subarashee* すばらしい！
Wonderful food!	*Oi-shee* おいしい！
It's really nice here!	*Tanoshee des-ne* 楽しいですねえ！

How nice!	*Steki*
	すてき！
How pretty!	*Kiray*
	きれい！
How nice for you!	*Ee des-ne*
	いいですね。
I'm very happy with...	*... ni manzoku shitay imas*
	…に満足しています。
I'm not very happy with...	*... ni manzoku shitay imasen*
	…に満足していません。
I'm glad...	*... ureshee*
	…うれしい。
I'm having a great time	*Totemo tanoshinde imas*
	とても楽しんでいます。
I'm looking forward to it	*Soray-o tanoshimi-ni mattay-imas*
	それを楽しみに待っています。
That's great	*Sugoi*
	すごい！
What a pity!	*Zannen*
	残念！
That's ridiculous!	*Baka-baka-shee*
	ばかばかしい！
What nonsense/How silly!	*Bakara-shee*
	ばからしい！
I don't like...	*... wa ki-righ des*
	…は嫌いです。
I'm bored to death	*Unzari da-yo*
	うんざりだよ。
I've had enough	*Moh akita*
	もうあきた。
This is no good	*Damay (da) yo*
	だめ（だ）よ。

3 Small Talk

3. Small Talk

 Introductions

May I introduce myself?	*Jiko shohkigh shtay-mo yoroshee des-ka* 自己紹介してもよろしいですか。
My name's...	*Watashi-wa... des* 私は…です。
What's your name?	*Onama-e-wa* お名前は？
May I introduce...?	*Chotto go-shohkigh shimas, ... san des* ちょっとご紹介します。…さんです。
This is my wife	*Kore-wa tsuma des* これは妻です。
This is my daughter	*Kore-wa musumay des* これは娘です。
This is my mother	*Kore-wa haha des* これは母です。
This is my friend	*Kore-wa tomodachi des* これは友達です。
This is my husband	*Kore-wa otto des* これは夫です。
This is my son	*Kore-wa musko des* これは息子です。
This is my father	*Kore-wa chichi des* これは父です。
How do you do	*Hajime-mashtay, dohzo yoroshku* 初めまして。どうぞよろしく。
Pleased to meet you	*Omay-ni kakaretay ureshee des* お目にかかれて嬉しいです。
Where are you from?	*Okuni-wa dochira des-ka* お国はどちらですか。

I'm from the U.S.A.	*Amerika desu* アメリカです。
What city do you live in?	*Doko-ni osu-migh des-ka* どこにお住まいですか。
In...	*... ni* …に
It's near...	*Soray-wa ... ni chi-kigh tokoro des* それは…に近い所です。
Have you been here long?	*Moh onagai no des-ka* もうお長いのですか。
A few days	*Ni san nichi des* 二三日です。
How long are you staying here?	*Dono gurigh koko-ni oraremas-ka* どのぐらいここにおられますか。
We're leaving tomorrow	*Ashta tachimas* 明日立ちます。
We're probably leaving in two weeks	*Nishookan-go ni tatsu tsumori des* 二週間後に立つつもりです。
Where are you staying?	*Doko-ni otomari des-ka* どこにお泊りですか。
In a hotel	*Hoteru-ni* ホテルに
With friends	*Tomodachi-no tokoro-ni* 友達の所に
With relatives	*Shinseki-no tokoro-ni* 親戚の所に
Are you here on your own?	*Shtori-day koraremashta-ka* 一人で来られましたか。
Are you here with your family?	*Gokazoku-to koko-ni kimashta-ka* ご家族とここに来ましたか。
I'm on my own	*Shtori des* 一人です。
I'm with my wife	*Tsuma-to kimashta* 妻と来ました。

I'm with my husband	*Otto-to kimashta* 夫と来ました。
I'm with my family	*Kazoku-to kimashta* 家族と来ました。
I'm with a friend/friends	*Tomodachi-to kimashta* 友達と来ました。
Are you married?	*Kekkon shtay imas-ka* 結婚していますか。
Do you have a steady boyfriend/girlfriend?	*Koi-bito wa imas-ka* 恋人はいますか。
(female) That's none of your business	*(f) kankay-na-i desho* 関係ないでしょ！
(male) That's none of your business	*(m) kankay-na-i daroh* 関係ないだろ！
I'm married	*Kekkon shtay imasu* 結婚しています。
– single	*doku shin des* 独身です。
– separated/divorced	*rikon shtay imas* 離婚しています。
– a widow/widower	*miboh-jin/yamomay des* 未亡人／やもめです。
I live with someone	*Koibito-to sunday imas* 恋人と住んでいます。
Do you have any children?	*Oko-san-wa* お子さんは？
Do you have any grandchildren?	*Omago-san-wa* お孫さんは？
How old are you?	*Shitsuray des-nga, oikutsu des-ka* 失礼ですが、おいくつですか。
How old is she?	*Onna-no-ko wa ikutsu des-ka* 女の子はいくつですか。
How old is he?	*Otoko-no-ko wa ikutsu des-ka* 男の子はいくつですか。

I'm...	...sigh des …歳です。
She's/he's...	...sigh des …歳です。
What do you do for a living?	Oshigoto-wa nan des-ka お仕事は何ですか。
I work in an office	Kighsha-de hata-right-tay imas 会社で働いています。
I'm a student/ I'm at school	Gaksay des 学生です。
I'm unemployed	Mushoku des 無職です。
I'm retired	Tigh-shoku shimashta 退職しました。
I'm on a disability pension	Shoh-gigh-sha des 障害者です。
I'm a housewife	Shufu des 主婦です。
Do you like your job?	O-shigoto-wa omoshiroi des-ka お仕事は面白いですか。
Most of the time	Tigh-gigh-wa たいがいは。
I usually do, but I prefer vacations	Mah mah des-nga, yasumi-no hoh-nga omoshiroi des-yo-ne まあまあですが、休みの方が面白いですよね。

3.2 I beg your pardon?

I don't speak any	Zen-zen ha-nasay-masen ぜんぜん話せません。
I speak a little...	Skoshi dakay ... ha-nasay-mas 少しだけ…話せます。

I'm American	*Watashi-wa Amerika-jin des* 私はアメリカ人です。
Do you speak English?	*Aygo/-wa hanasay-mas-ka* 英語は話せますか。
Can you speak Japanese?	*Nihongo wo hanasay mas-ka?* 日本語が話せますか。
Can you speak English?	*Eigo wa hanasay mas-ka?* 英語が話せますか。
Is there anyone who speaks...?	*Koko ni-wa ... ga hanaseru shto-ga imas-ka* ここには…が話せる人がいますか。
I beg your pardon?	*Nan-to ossha-i-mashta-ka* 何とおっしゃいましたか。
I understand	*Wakarimashta* 分かりました。
I don't understand	*Chotto wakarimasen* ちょっと分かりません。
Do you understand me?	*Wakarimas-ka* 分かりますか。
Could you repeat that, please?	*Moh ichido ittay kuda-sigh* もう一度言って下さい。
Could you speak more slowly, please?	*Yukkuri hanashtay kudasai-masen-ka* ゆっくり話して下さいませんか。
What does that mean?	*Soray-wa doh yoo imi des-ka* それはどういう意味ですか。
What does that word mean?	*Sono kotoba-wa doh yoo imi des-ka* その言葉はどういう意味ですか。
Is that similar to/ the same as...?	*Soray-wa... to yoo imi des-ka* それは…という意味ですか。
Could you point that out in this phrase book, please?	*Kono hon-no naka-de sore-o yubi-sashtay kudasa-i-masen-ka* この本の中でそれを指さして下さいませんか。
Could you write that down for me, please?	*Soray-o kaitay kudasa-i-masen-ka* それを書いて下さいませんか。

One moment, please, I have to look it up	*Chotto mattay kudasa-i, sagashtay mimas* ちょっと待って下さい、捜してみます。
I can't find the word	*Kotoba-ga mitsukarimasen* 言葉が見つかりません。
How do you say that in Japanese?	*Soray-wa nihongo-de doh ee-mas-ka* それは日本語でどう言いますか。
How do you pronounce that?	*Soray-wa doh hatsuon shimas-ka* それはどう発音しますか。

3.3 Starting/ending a conversation

Excuse me	*Sumimasen-nga* すみませんが
Excuse me, could you help me?	*Sumimasen-nga, tasketay kuda-sigh* すみませんが、助けて下さい。
Yes, what's the problem?	*Doh shimashta-ka* どうしましたか。
What can I do for you?	*Nani-ka goyoh deshoh-ka* 何かご用でしょうか。
Sorry, I don't have time now	*Isogimas noday, sumimasen* 急ぎますので、すみません。
Do you have a light?	*Hi-o mochi des-ka* 火をおもちですか。
May I join you?	*Golssho sasete Itadigh-tay-mo yoroshee des-ka* ご一緒させていただいてもよろしいですか。
Could you take a picture of me/us?	*Shashin-o tottay kudasaimas-ka* 写真をとってくださいますか。
Press this button	*Kono botan-o oshtay kuda-sigh* このボタンを押して下さい。
(female) Leave me alone	*(f) Hotto itay-yo* ほっといてよ！

(male) Leave me alone	*(m) Hotto itay kuray-yo* ほっといてくれよ！
(female) Get lost	*(f) Achi ittay-yo* あっちいってよ！
(male) Get lost	*(m) Achi ikay-yo* あっちいけよ！
(female) Go away or I'll scream	*(f) Ikanai-to, sakebu-wa-yo* 行かないと叫ぶわよ！
(male) Go away or I'll yell	*(m) Ikanai-to, sakebu-yo* 行かないと叫ぶよ！

 3.4 A chat about the weather

See also 1.5 The weather

It's so hot today!	*Kyoh-wa atsui des-ne* 今日は暑いですね。
It's so cold today!	*Kyoh-wa samui des-ne* 今日は寒いですね。
Nice weather, isn't it?	*Ee tenki des-ne* いい天気ですね。
What a wind!	*Sugoi kazay des-ne* すごい風ですね。
All that rain!	*Sugoi amay des-ne* すごい雨ですね。
All that snow!	*Yuki-wa sugoi des-ne* 雪が凄いですね。
All that fog!	*Fukigh kiri des-ne* 深い霧ですね。
Has the weather been like this for long here?	*Kono tenki-wa moh nagai-n des-ka* この天気はもう長いんですか。
Is it always this hot here?	*Kono hen-wa itsumo atsui-n des-ka* この辺はいつも暑いんですか。
Is it always this cold here?	*Kono hen-wa itsumo samui-n des-ka* この辺はいつも寒いんですか。

| Is it always this dry here? | *Kono hen-wa itsumo amay-nga sukunai-n des-ka*
この辺はいつも雨が少ないんですか。 |
| Is it always this wet here? | *Kono hen-wa itsumo amay-nga oh-ee des-ka*
この辺はいつも雨が多いですか。 |

3.5 Hobbies

Do you have any hobbies?	*Shoomi-wa* 趣味は？
I like knitting	*Amimono-ga ski des* 編みものが好きです。
I like reading	*Dokusho-ga ski des* 読書が好きです。
I like photography	*Shashin-o toru-no-ga ski de* 写真をとるのが好きです。
I like music	*Ongaku-ga ski des* 音楽が好きです。
I like playing the guitar	*Gitah-o hiku-no-ga ski des* ギターを弾くのが好きです。
I like playing the piano	*Piano-o hiku-no-ga ski des* ピアノを弾くのが好きです。
I like going to the movies	*Ayga-o mi-ni iku-no-ga ski des* 映画を見に行くのが好きです。
I like travelling	*Ryokoh suru-no-ga ski des* 旅行するのが好きです。
I like playing sports	*Spohtsu-ga ski des* スポーツが好きです。
I like fishing	*Tsuri-ni iku-no-ga ski des* つりに行くのが好きです。
I like walking	*Sampo suru-no-ga ski des* 散歩するのが好きです。

3.6 Invitations

Are you doing anything tonight?	*Moh komban-no yotay-wa nani-ka kimeta-no* もう今晩の予定は何か決めたの。
Do you have any plans for today?	*Moh kyoh-no kaykaku-wa tatemashta-ka* もう今日の計画はたてましたか。
Do you have any plans for tonight?	*Moh komban-no kaykaku-wa tatemashta-ka* もう今晩の計画はたてましたか。
Would you like to go out with me?	*Isshoh-ni dekakemasen-ka* 一緒に出かけませんか。
Would you like to go dancing with me?	*Isshoh-ni dansu-ni ikimasen-ka* 一緒にダンスに行きませんか。
Would you like to have lunch/dinner with me?	*Isshoh-ni tabemasen-ka* 一緒に食べませんか。
Would you like to come to the beach with me?	*Isshoh-ni kighgan-ni ikimasen-ka* 一緒に海岸に行きませんか。
Would you like to come into town with us?	*Isshoh-ni machi-e ikimasen-ka* 一緒に町へ行きませんか。
Would you like to come and see some friends with us?	*isshoh-ni tomodachi-no tokoro-ni ikimasen-ka* 一緒に友達の所に行きませんか。
I don't dance	*Odorimasen* 踊りません。
Shall we sit at the bar?	*Bah-ni suwari-masho-ka* バーに座りましょうか？
Shall we get something to drink?	*Nani-ka nomi-mashoh-ka* 何か飲みましょうか。
Shall we go for a walk?	*Sampoh-ni iki-mashoh-ka* 散歩に行きましょうか。
Shall we go for a drive?	*Drighb-ni iki-mashoh-ka* ドライブに行きましょうか。

Small Talk

3

Yes, all right	*Ee-ne* いいね。
Good idea	*Ee kangae* いい考え
No (thank you)	*Ee-ye, kekkoh des* いいえ、けっこうです
Maybe later	*Tabun kondo* 多分今度。
(female) I don't feel like it	*(f) Kyohmi-nga nigh-wa* 興味がないわ。
(male) I don't feel like it	*(m) Kyohmi-nga nigh-yo* 興味がないよ。
(female) I don't have time	*(f) Jikan-nga nigh-wa* 時間がないわ。
(male) I don't have time	*(m) Jikan-nga nigh-yo* 時間がないよ。
I already have a date	*Moh hoka-no yakusoku-nga* もう他の約束が。
I'm not very good at dancing	*Dans-wa heta-des* ダンスは下手です。
I'm not very good at volleyball	*Baray-bohru-wa heta-des* バレーボールは下手です。
I can't swim	*Oyogemasen* 泳げません。

3.7 Paying a compliment

You look wonderful!	*Okiray des-ne* おきれいですね。
I like your car!	*Ee kuruma des-ne* いい車ですね！
What a sweet child!	*Nantay kawa-ee akachan deshoh* 何てかわいい赤ちゃんでしょう。

You're a wonderful dancer!	*Dans-ga johzu des-ne* ダンスが上手ですね。
You're a wonderful cook!	*Ryohri-ga johzu des-ne* 料理が上手ですね。
You're a terrific tennis player!	*Tenisu-ga johzu des-ne* テニスが上手ですね。

3.8 Intimate comments/questions

I like being with you	*Isshoh-ni iru-no-ga tanoshee* 一緒にいるのが楽しい。
(female) I've missed you so much	*(f) Tottemo sabishikatta-wa* とっても寂しかったわ。
(male) I've missed you so much	*(m) Tottemo sabishikatta-yo* とっても寂しかったよ。
(female) I dreamt about you	*(f) Anata-o yumay-ni mita-wa* あなたを夢にみたわ。
(male) I dreamt about you	*(m) Kimi-o yumay-ni mita-yo* 君を夢にみたよ。
You're pretty!	*Kiray da-yo* きれいだよ。
(female) You're nice	*(f) Steki-yo* すてきよ。
(male) You're nice	*(m) Steki da-yo* すてきだよ。
You're sexy	*Sekshee* セクシー。
(female) Look at me	*(f) Watashi-o mitay* 私を見て。
(male) Look at me	*(m) Boku-o mitay* 僕を見て。
You have such beautiful eyes	*Kiray-na shtomi da-ne* きれいな瞳だね。

(female) I'm crazy about you	*(f) Anata-ni muchoo na no* あなたに夢中なの。
(male) I'm crazy about you	*(m) Kimi-ni muchoo nanda* 君に夢中なんだ。
I love you	*Igh-shteru* 愛してる。
(female) I love you too	*(f) Watashi-mo* 私も。
(male) I love you too	*(m) Boku-mo* 僕も。
(female) I don't feel as strongly about you	*(f) Watashi-no kimochi-wa chigau-no* 私の気持ちは違うの。
(male) I don't feel as strongly about you	*(m) Boku-no kimochi-wa chigaun-da* 僕の気持ちは違うんだ。
I already have a boyfriend/girlfriend	*Moh koibito-ga imas* もう恋人がいます。
I'm not ready for that	*Moh skoshi mattay* もう少し待って。
(female) This is going too fast for me	*(f) Sugoku haya-sugiru-no* すごく早過ぎるの。
(male) This is going too fast for me	*(m) Sugoku haya-sugiru-yo* すごく早過ぎるよ。
(female) Take your hands off me	*(f) Sawara-nigh-day* 触らないで。
Okay, no problem	*Ee-yo* いいよ。
Will you stay with me tonight?	*Konya issoh-ni tomara-nigh?* 今夜一緒に泊まらない？
I'd like to go to bed with you	*Igh-shtigh* 愛したい。
Only if we use a condom	*Kondom-o tsukattay kureru-nara* コンドームを使ってくれるなら。
We have to be careful about AIDS	*Ayzu-no koto-mo aru kara-ne* エイズのこともあるからね。

(female) That's what they all say	(f) Otokot-tay mina soh yoo no-ne 男って皆そういうのね。
(female) We shouldn't take any risks	(f) Kiken-wa sakay mashoh-yo 危険は避けましょうよ。
(male) We shouldn't take any risks	(m) Kiken-wa sakay-yoh-yo 危険は避けようよ。
Do you have a condom?	Kondom motteru? コンドームもってる？
(female) No? In that case we won't do it	(f) Sore-nara, yamemashoh それなら、やめましょう。
(male) No? In that case we won't do it	(m) Sore-nara, yameyoh それなら、やめよう。

3.9 Congratulations and condolences

| Happy birthday/many happy returns | Otanjohbi omedetoh gozaimas
お誕生日おめでとうございます。 |
| Please accept my condolences | Kokoro-kara o-kuyami mohshi-agemas
心からお悔やみ申し上げます。 |

3.10 Arrangements

When will I see you again?	Kondo itsu aemas-ka 今度いつ会えますか。
Are you free over the weekend?	Kono shoomatsu ohima des-ka この週末おひまですか。
What shall we do?	Nani-ka kay-kaku shimashoh-ka 何か計画しましょうか。
Where shall we meet?	Doko-de aimashoh-ka どこで会いましょうか。
Will you pick me/us up?	Kuruma-de hirottay kudasaimas-ka 車で拾ってくださいますか。
Shall I pick you up?	Kuruma-de hirottay agemashoh-ka 車で拾って上げましょうか。

I have to be home by...	...ji-made-ni kaera-nakeraba-narimasen …時までに帰らなければなりません。
(female) I don't want to see you anymore	(f) Moh aitaku-nigh-wa もう会いたくないわ。
(male) I don't want to see you anymore	(m) Moh aitaku-nigh-yo もう会いたくないよ。

3.11 Being the host(ess)

See also 4 Eating out

Can I offer you a drink?	Nani-ka onomi-ni-narimasen-ka 何かお飲みになりませんか。
What would you like to drink?	Nani-o onomi-ni narimas-ka 何をお飲みになりますか。
Would you like a cigarette?	Tabako-wa ikaga des-ka タバコはいかがですか。
Would you like a cigar?	Hamaki-wa ikaga des-ka 葉巻はいかがですか。
Something non-alcoholic, please	Arukohru-nashi no nomimono-o kuda-sigh アルコールなしの飲み物を下さい。
I don't smoke	Tabako-wa suimasen たばこは吸いません。

3.12 Saying good-bye

Can I take you home?	Okuttay ittay-mo ee des-ka 送っていってもいいですか。
Can I write?	Tegami-o kaitay-mo ee des-ka 手紙を書いてもいいですか。
Can I email you?	May-ru wo shite-mo e-des-ka メールをしてもいいですか。
Can I call you?	Denwa-o kaketay-mo ee des-ka 電話をかけてもいいですか。

Will you write to me?	*Tegami-o kuremas-ka* 手紙をくれますか。
Will you call me?	*Denwa-o kuremas-ka* 電話をくれますか。
Can I have your address?	*Anata-no joosho-o oshietay kuremas-ka* あなたの住所を教えてくれますか。
Can I have your phone number?	*Anata-no denwa bango-o oshietay kuremas-ka* あなたの電話番号を教えてくれますか。
May I know your email address?	*Me-ru adores-wo oshiete kuda-sigh* メールアドレスを教えてください。
Thanks for everything	*Iro-iro arigatoh goza-i-mashta* いろいろありがとうございました。
It was very nice	*Totemo tanoshikatta des* とても楽しかったです。
Say hello to...	*... san ni yoroshku* …さんによろしく。
All the best	*Genki de-ne* 元気でね。
When will you be back?	*Itsu kaeru?* いつ帰る？
(female) I'll be waiting for you	*(f) Matteru-wa* 待ってるわ。
(male) I'll be waiting for you	*(m) Matteru-yo* 待ってるよ。
(female) I'd like to see you again	*(f) Mata ai-tigh-wa* また会いたいわ。
(male) I'd like to see you again	*(m) Mata ai-tigh-nah* また会いたいなあ。
This is our address. If you're ever in the U.S., you'd be more than welcome	*Watashi-tachi-no joosho des. itsu-demo Amerika-ni irashtara dohzo* 私たちの住所です。いつでもアメリカにいらしたらどうぞ。

4 Eating out

4. Eating out

● **Large cities like Tokyo** offer a vast selection of restaurants with food from all over the world. American fast food chain outlets can be found in most neighborhoods near railway stations. Very popular too are "family restaurants", where wide-ranging menus offer budget-priced dishes to suit the whole family. All department stores have two or more restaurant floors, with individual restaurants serving most varieties of Japanese, Chinese, and Western food. In addition there is usually a large customers' restaurant, again with a wide selection. Food selection is made very easy in Japan because all restaurants display in their window wax models of the dishes offered and their prices. Family restaurants provide a fully-illustrated menu. Only very expensive, upscale restaurants do not do this. Children are almost always welcome at local restaurants and those in the popular shopping centers and stations. Traditional restaurants with tatami (straw-matted) floors are a benefit for those with babies.

4.1 At the restaurant

I'd like to reserve a table for seven o'clock, please	*Shichiji-ni tehburu-o yoyaku shi-tigh no des-nga* 七時にテーブルを予約したいのですが。
I'd like a table for two, please	*Futari-yoh-no tehburu-o onegigh shimas* 二人用のテーブルをお願いします。
We've reserved	*Yoyaku shimashta* 予約しました。
We haven't reserved	*Yoyaku shtay imasen* 予約していません。
What time does the restaurant open	*Restoran-wa nanji-kara ohpen des-ka* レストランは何時からオープンですか。
What time does the restaurant close?	*Restoran-wa nanji maday des-ka* レストランは何時まででですか。

ご予約ですか	Do you have a reservation?
お名前は	What name, please?
喫煙席と禁煙席、どちらになさいますか。	Smoking or non-smoking?
喫煙席をお願いします。	Smoking, please
禁煙席をお願いします。	Non-smoking, please
こちらへ	This way, please
このテーブルは予約済みです。	This table is reserved
15分お待ちいただくとテーブルが空きます。	We'll have a table free in fifteen minutes
(バーで)お待ちになりますか	Would you like to wait (at the bar)?

Can we wait for a table?	*Tehburu-ga aku-made machi-tigh no des-nga* テーブルが空くまで待ちたいのですが。
Do we have to wait long?	*Nagaku machimas-ka* 長く待ちますか。
Is this seat taken?	*Kono seki ightay imas-ka* この席、空いてますか。
Could we sit here?	*Koko-ni suwatte-mo ee des-ka* ここに座ってもいいですか。
Could we sit there?	*Asoko-ni suwatte-mo ee des-ka* あそこに座ってもいいですか。
Can we sit by the window?	*Mado-giwa-ni suwatte mo ee des-ka* 窓ぎわに座ってもいいですか。
Can we eat outside?	*Soto demo taberaremas-ka* 外でも食べられますか。
Do you have another chair for us?	*Isu moh ikko arimas-ka* 椅子もう一個ありますか。
Do you have a highchair?	*Kodomo-yoh-no isu-ga arimas-ka* 子供用の椅子がありますか。

Could you warm up this bottle/jar for me?	*Sumimasen-ga, kono bin-o tatametay kuremas-ka* すみませんが、このびんを暖めてくれますか。
Not too hot, please	*Atsu-stuginigh yoh-ni onegai shimasu* 熱過ぎないようにお願いします。
Is there somewhere I can change the baby's diaper?	*Bebee-room arimas-ka* ベビールームありますか。
Where are the restrooms?	*Toireh-wa doko des-ka* トイレはどこですか。

4.2 Ordering

Waiter!	*Wehtah-san!* ウェーターさん
Waitress!	*Wehtres-san!* ウェートレスさん
We'd like something to eat	*Nani-ka tabe-tigh-n des-nga* 何か食べたいんですが。
We'd like a drink	*Nani-ka nomi-tigh-n des-nga* 何か飲みたいんですが。
Could I have a quick meal?	*Nani-ka hayaku dekiru shina-wa arimas-ka* 何か速く出来る品はありますか。
We don't have much time	*Isoiday iru no des-nga* 急いでいるのですが。
We'd like to have a drink first	*Mazu nani-ka nomi-tig-n des-nga* 先ず何か飲みたいんですが
Do you have a menu in English?	*Aygo no menyoo-wa arimas-ka* 英語のメニューはありますか。
Do you have a dish of the day?	*Kyoh no menyoo-wa arimas-ka* 今日のメニューはありますか。
We haven't made a choice yet	*Mada kimarimasen* まだ決りません。

What do you recommend?	*O-susume-hin-wa nan des-ka* お薦め品は何ですか。
What are the specials?	*Tokubetsu ryohri-wa nan des-ka* 特別料理は何ですか。
I don't like...	*... wa ski ja nigh-n des* …は好きじゃないんです。
I don't like fish	*Sakana-wa ski ja nigh-n des* 魚は好きじゃないんです。
I don't like meat	*Niku-wa ski ja nigh-n des* 肉は好きじゃないんです。
What's this?	*Koray-wa nan des-ka* これは何ですか。
Does it have...in it?	*... nga ha-ittay imas-ka* …が入っていますか。
Is this a hot dish?	*Kono ryohri-wa atata-kigh des-ka* この料理は暖かいですか。
Is this a cold dish?	*Kono ryohri-wa tsume-tigh des-ka* この料理は冷たいですか。
Is this sweet?	*Kono ryohri-wa a-migh des-ka* この料理は甘いですか。
Is this spicy?	*Kono ryohri-wa ka-righ des-ka* この料理はからいですか。
Do you have anything else, please?	*Hoka-ni nani-ka arimas-ka* 他に何かありますか。
I'm on a salt-free diet	*Sheeo-nuki-de onegai-shimas* 塩ぬきでお願いします。
I can't eat pork	*Butaniku-wa taberare-masen* 豚肉は食べられません。
– sugar	*Satoh-wa taberare-masen* 砂糖は食べられません。
– fatty foods	*Aburap-poy ryohri-wa taberare-masen* 油っぽい料理は食べられません。
– (hot) spices	*(Karigh) spighs-wa taberare-masen* （辛い）スパイスは食べられません。

I'll/we'll have what those people are having — *Ano-shto-to onaji ryohri-o onegai-shimas*
あの人と同じ料理を、お願いします。

I'd like... — *... onegai-shimas*
…お願いします。

Do you have a knife and fork? — *Nighf to fohk arimas-ka*
ナイフとフォークありますか。

A little more rice please — *Gohan moh skoshi onegigh-shimas*
ご飯もう少しお願いします。

Another glass of water, please — *Mizu moh ip-pigh onegigh-shimas*
水もう一杯お願いします。

One more please — *Moh hitotsu onegigh-shimas*
もう一つお願いします。

Do you have salt and pepper? — *Sheeo to koshoh arimas-ka*
塩と胡椒ありますか。

Do you have a napkin? — *Napukin arimas-ka*
ナプキンありますか。

Do you have a spoon? — *Spoon arimas-ka*
スプーンありますか。

Do you have an ashtray? — *High-zara arimas-ka*
灰皿ありますか。

Do you have any matches? — *Match arimas-ka*
マッチありますか。

Do you have any toothpicks? — *Tsuma-yohji arimas-ka*
つまようじありますか。

Can I have a glass of water, please — *Mizu ippigh onegigh-shimas*
水一杯お願いします。

Do you have a straw? — *Stroh arimas-ka*
ストローありますか。

Let's begin — *Itadakimashoh*
いただきましょう。

Cheers! — *Kam-pigh*
乾杯

The next round's on me — *Kondo-wa watashi-nga ogorimas*
今度は私がおごります。

It's on me today.
(It's my treat.)
kyoh-wa watashi no ogori des
今日は私のおごりです。

Thank you for the meal.
Gochi soh sama deshta
ごちそうさまでした。

4.3 The bill

See also 8.2 Settling the bill

How much is this dish?
Kono ryohri-wa ikura des-ka
この料理はいくらですか。

Could I have the bill,
please?
Okanjoh onegigh-shimas
お勘定、お願いします。

All together
Zembu-de
全部で

Separate checks, please
Betsu-betsu de onegigh-shimas
別々でお願いします。

Could we have the
menu again, please?
*Moh ik-kigh menyoo-o misetay
kuda-sigh*
もう一回メニューを見せて下さい。

The...is not on the bill
... ga hight-tay imasen
…が入っていません。

4.4 Complaints

It's taking a very long
time
Zuibun nagaku kakattay imas-ne
ずいぶん長くかかっていますね。

We've been here an
hour already
Moh ichi-jikan-mo mattay imas
もう一時間も待っています。

This must be a mistake
Koray-wa machigigh deshoh
これは間違いでしょう。

This is not what I
ordered
Koray-wa choomon shimasen deshta
これは注文しませんでした。

I ordered...
... o choomon shimashta
…を注文しました。

There's a dish missing	*Ryohri-ga ippin fusoku des* 料理が一品不足です。
This is broken	*Kore-wa kowarete-imas* これは壊れています。
This is not clean	*Chotto koray kita-nigh no des-nga* ちょっとこれきたないのですが。
The food's cold	*Ryohri-ga tsume-tigh-n des* 料理が冷たいんです。
– not fresh	*Koray-wa shinsen ja nigh des* これは新鮮じゃないです。
– too salty	*Koray-wa sheeo ka-righ des* これは塩辛いです。
– too sweet	*Koray-wa ama-sugimas* これは甘過ぎます。
– too spicy	*Koray-wa kara-sugimas* これは辛過ぎます。
The meat's not done	*Niku-wa yaki-tarimasen* 肉は焼き足りません。
– overdone	*Niku-wa yaki-sugi des* 肉は焼き過ぎです。
– tough	*Niku-ga ka-tigh-n des* 肉が堅いんです。
– spoiled	*Niku-ga kusattay imas* 肉がくさっています。
Could I have something else instead of this?	*Kawari-no shina-o kudasai-masen-ka* 代わりの品を下さいませんか。
The bill/this amount is not right	*Kanjoh-nga aimasen* 勘定が合いません。
We didn't have this	*Koray-wa tabe-masen deshta* これは食べませんでした。
There's no paper in the restroom	*Toiretto-pehpah-ga nigh-n des* トイレットペーパーがないんです。
Will you get the manager, please?	*Sekinin-sha-o yonday kuda-sigh* 責任者を呼んでください。

4.5 Paying a compliment

That was a wonderful meal
Totemo oishikatta-des
とてもおいしかったです。

The food was excellent
Gochisoh sama deshta
ごちそうさまでした。

The...in particular was delicious
Toku-ni ... nga totemo oishikatta-des
特に…がとてもおいしかったです。

4.6 The menu

The following are some of the most popular Japanese dishes.

しゃぶしゃぶ   *Shabu shabu*
Thin strips of pork or lamb and various vegetables cooked in front of you in boiling water and eaten in dipping sauces.

焼き鳥   *Yakitori*
Marinated chicken pieces on skewers, cooked over a brazier.

味噌汁   *Misoshiru*
Soup made from miso (paste of fermented soy beans) with tofu and vegetables such as cabbage and small mushrooms.

うどん、そば   *Udon, soba*
Thick white and thin brown noodles respectively. Served either cold with dipping sauces (good in summer) or warm in a soup.

茶わんむし   *Chawan-mushi*
Fish and vegetables steamed in an egg custard.

豚カツ   *Tonkatsu*
Pork cutlets fried in breadcrumbs and served with a thick brown sauce.

親子どんぶり   *Oyako donburi*
Chicken and egg served on rice. A popular lunch dish.

カレーライス   *Karee raisu (karay righ-su)*
The Japanese version of curry and rice. Usually beef, chicken, or pork pieces in a curry sauce.

お好み焼き　　　　　*Okonomi yaki*

A Japanese pancake containing a variety of ingredients, such as vegetables, meat and seafood. *Okonomiyaki* originally came from the Hiroshima area of Japan, but is widely available throughout the country. Toppings and batters tend to vary according to region.

おにぎり　　　　　*Onigiri*

Also known as *omusubi* (おむすび) or rice ball, is a Japanese food made from white rice formed into triangular or oval shapes and often wrapped in *nori* (seaweed). Traditionally, an *onigiri* is filled with pickled *ume* (umeboshi), salted salmon, *katsuobushi*, *kombu*, *tarako*, or any other salty or sour ingredient as a natural preservative. Because of the popularity of *onigiri* in Japan, most convenience stores stock *onigiri* with various fillings and flavors. There are even specialized shops whose only products are *onigiri* for takeout.

オムライス　　　　　*Omurice*

Chicken ketchup rice wrapped in a thin sheet of fried egg and usually topped with ketchup. This dish is also highly popular with children and often featured on kids' menus.

焼きそば　　　　　*Yakisoba*

Literally means "fried noodles." It has ramen-style noodles, bite-sized pork, cabbage, onions and carrots flavored with *yakisoba* sauce. It is often sold at festivals in Japan.

焼き肉　　　　　*Yakiniku*

Means "grilled meat" and is similar to what is known as Korean barbecue. Today, it commonly refers to a Japanese style of cooking bite-sized meat (usually beef and offal) and vegetables on griddles over flame of a kind of wood charcoal (*sumibi* 炭火) or gas/electric grill.

寿司　　　　　*Sushi*

Raw or cooked fish, vegetables, or various other ingredients over rice seasoned with rice vinegar, Sushi is the most famous Japanese dish outside of Japan, and one of the most popular dishes among the Japanese themselves. In Japan, sushi is usually enjoyed on special occasions, such as a celebration.

5 Getting Around

5. Getting Around

5.1 Asking directions

Excuse me, could I ask you something?	*Sumimasen-nga* すみませんが
I've lost my way	*Michi-ni mayottay shimattan-des-nga* 道に迷ってしまったんですが。
Is there a(n)... around here?	*Kono hen-ni ... ga arimas-ka* この辺に…がありますか。
Is this the way to...?	*Kono michi-wa ... e ikimas-ka* この道は…へ行きますか。
Could you tell me how to get to the... (name of place) by car/on foot?	*... e doh iku-ka oshietay kudasai-masen-ka* …へどう行くか教えて下さいませんか。
What's the quickest way to...?	*E no ichiban no chika-michi wa oh ikimas-ka* …への一番の近道はどう行きますか。
How many kilometers is it to...?	*... maday nankiro-gurigh-n des-ka* …まで何キロぐらいですか。
Could you point it out on the map?	*Kono chizu-de yubi-sashtay kuda-sigh* この地図で指差して下さい。
My children are entered on this passport	*Kodomo-wa kono pas-pohto-ni kinyoo shitay arimas* 子供はこのパスポートに記入してあります。

すみませんが、わかりません。	I am sorry, but I don't know my way around here
道が違います。	You're going the wrong way
…に戻らなければなりません。	You have to go back to...
そこに着いたら、もう一度尋ねて ください。	When you get there, ask again

真っ直ぐ straight ahead	信号 traffic light	高架橋 overpass	左に left
交差点 intersection	トンネル tunnel	橋 bridge	右に right
道 street	一旦停止標識 'yield'	矢印 arrow	渡って cross
踏切 grade crossing/ barrier gates	曲がり角で at the corner	建物／ビル building	川 river

 The car

See the diagram on page 67

An international driving license is required to drive in Japan.
Traffic drives on the left. The speed limit varies but is usually
around 40 kph in urban areas and 80 kph on highways; it is 100
kph on highways. Driving can be complicated because, on some
of the highways, signs are written in Japanese characters. Highways are expensive, and there are many toll roads, especially in
scenic areas.

 The gas station

How many kilometers
  to the next gas station,
  please?
	Tsugi-no gasorin-sutando-maday
	nankiro gurigh des-ka
	次のガソリン・スタンドまで何キロぐ
	らいですか。

I would like...liters of..., please	*... o ...rittoru onegigh-shimas* …を…リットルお願いします。
– super	*high-oku* ハイオク
– leaded	*yoo-en* 有鉛

The parts of a car

(the diagram shows the numbered parts)

1	battery	バッテリー	*batteree*
2	rear light	バック・ライト	*bakku-right*
3	rear-view mirror	バック・ミラー	*bakku-mirah*
	backup light	バックアップ・ライト	*bakku-upp-right*
4	antenna	アンテナ	*antena*
	car radio	ラジオ	*rajio*
5	gas tank	燃料タンク／ガソリン・タンク	*nenryoh-tanku/gasorin-tanku*
6	spark plugs	スパーク・プラグ	*spahk puragu*
	fuel filter/pump	燃料フィルター／ ポンプ	*nenryoh firutah/pomp*
7	side mirror	サイド・ミラー	*sighdo-mirah*
8	bumper	バンパー	*banpah*
	carburettor	キャブレター	*kyaburetah*
	crankcase	クランク・ケース	*krank-kays*
	cylinder	シリンダー	*shirindah*
	ignition	イグニッション	*igunishon*
	warning light	警告灯	*kay-koku-toh*
	generator	発電器	*hats-den-ki*
	accelerator	アクセル	*akuseru*
	handbrake	ハンドブレーキ	*hando-burayki*
	valve	弁／バルブ	*ben/barubu*
9	silencer	マフラー／消音器	*mufurah/shoh-on-ki*
10	trunk	トランク	*toranku*
11	headlight	ヘッド・ライト	*heddo-right*
	crank shaft	クランクシャフト	*kurank-shafuto*
12	air filter	エア・フィルター	*e-a firutah*
	fog lamp	フォグ・ランプ	*fog-rampu*
13	engine block	エンジン	*enjin*
	camshaft	カムシャフト	*kamu-shafuto*
	oil filter/pump	オイル・フィルター／ポンプ	*oyru-firutah/pomp*
	dipstick	オイルゲージ	*oyru-gayji*
	pedal	ペダル	*pedaru*
14	door	ドア	*do-a*
15	radiator	ラジエーター	*raji-aytah*
16	brake disc	ブレーキ・ディスク	*burayk-disk*
	spare wheel	スペア・タイヤ	*supe-a tigh-a*
17	indicator	方向指示器	*hohkoh-shijiki*
18	windshield wiper	ワイパー	*wigh-pah*
19	shock absorbers	ショック・アブソーバー	*shokk-absohbah*
	sunroof	サンルーフ	*sanroof*
	spoiler	スポイラー	*spoy-rah*
	starter motor	スターターモーター	*stahtah-mohtah*
20	steering column	ステアリング・コラム	*stearing-koram*
21	exhaust pipe	排気管	*high-ki-kan*
22	seat belt	シートベルト	*sheet-beruto*
	fan	ファン	*fan*

Getting Around

5

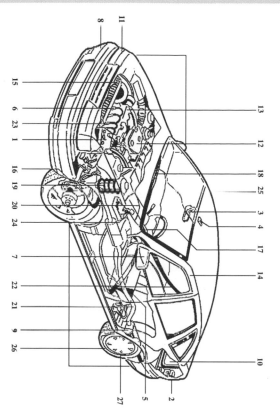

23	distributor cables	ディストリビューター・ケーブル	*distribyutah kayburu*
24	gear shift	シフト・レバー	*shift-rebah*
25	windshield water pump	フロントガラス ウォーターポンプ	*fronto-garas* *wohtah-pomp*
26	wheel	タイヤ	*tigh-yah*
27	hubcap piston	ハブ・キャップ ピストン	*hab-kyapp* *piston*

GPS(ジーピーエス)／ナビ/カーナビ GPS	ハイブリッドカー／車 hybrid car
グリーンカー green car	電気自動車 electric car

– unleaded	*mu-en* 無鉛
– diesel	*dee-zeru* ディーゼル
– regular gasoline	*regurah* レギュラー
I would like...yen's worth of gas, please	*...en bun dakay gasorin o-negigh-shimas* …円分だけガソリンお願いします。
Fill her up, please	*Mantan o-negigh-shimas* 満タンお願いします。
Could you check...?	*... o tenken shitay kuda-sigh* …を点検して下さい。
– the oil level	*oyru* オイル
– the tire pressure	*tighya-no kooki-ats* タイヤの空気圧
Could you change the oil, please?	*Oyru-o ka-etay kuremas-ka* オイルを替えてくれますか。
Could you clean the windows/the windshield, please?	*(fronto) Garas-o fu-itay kuremas-ka* (フロント)ガラスをふいてくれますか。
Could you wash the car, please?	*Sensha o-negigh-shimas* 洗車お願いします。

5.4 Breakdowns and repairs

I'm having car trouble. Could you give me a hand?	*Kuruma-nga koshoh shimashta. Tetsu-dattay kudasa-e-masen-ka* 車が故障しました。手伝ってください ませんか。
I've run out of gas	*Gasorin-ga nigh-n des-nga* ガソリンがないんですが

I've locked the keys in the car	*Kagl-o kuruma-no naka-ni wasuretay shima-imashta* 鍵を車の中に忘れてしまいました。
The car/motorcycle/ moped won't start	*Enjin-nga kakarimasen* エンジンがかかりません。
Could you call a garage for me, please?	*Shoori-ya-o yonday kuremasen-ka* 修理屋を呼んでくれませんか。
Could you give me a lift to...?	*... maday nosetay kudasa-e-masen-ka* …まで乗せて下さいませんか。
– a garage?	*shoori-ya* 修理屋
– into town?	*machi* 町
– a phone booth?	*denwa boks* 電話ボックス
Can we take my bicycle?	*Jitensha-mo mottay ikemas-ka* 自転車も持って行けますか。
– scooter	*Skootah-mo mottay ikemas-ka* スクーターも持って行けますか。
Could you tow me to a garage?	*Shoori-ya-maday kuruma-o hakonday kudasa-e-masen-ka* 修理屋まで車を運んで下さいませんか。
There's probably something wrong with... (See 5.2 and 5.5)	*... ga warui-n des-nga* …が悪いんですが。
Can you fix it?	*Shoori dekimas-ka* 修理できますか。
Could you fix my tire?	*Tigh-ya-o shoori shtay kuda-sigh* タイヤを修理して下さい。
Could you change this wheel?	*Kono tigh-ya-o kohkan shtay kuda-sigh* このタイヤを交換して下さい。
Can you fix it so it'll get me to...?	*... e ikeru maday-no shoori-o o-negigh-deki mas-ka* …へ行けるまでの修理をお願いできますか。

Which garage can help me?	*Dono shoori-ya-de shoori dekimas-ka* どの修理屋で修理出来ますか。
When will my car/ bicycle be ready?	*Its tori-ni koremas-ka* いつ取りに来れますか。
Can I wait for it here?	*Koko-de matemas-ka* ここで待てますか。
How much will it cost?	*Ikura kakarimas-ka* いくらかかりますか。
Could you itemize the bill?	*Kanjoh-o maysigh-ni kigh-tay kuda-sigh* 勘定を明細に書いて下さい。
Can I have a receipt for the insurance?	*Hoken-no tamay-no ryohshoo-sho-o kuda-sigh* 保険のための領収書を下さい。

5.5 Bicycles/mopeds

See the diagram on page 73

The bicycle is used by large numbers of commuters to get to stations and by housewives shopping in the local shopping districts. Because the roads are considered dangerous, most cyclists use footpaths; cycle paths are rare. Bicycles can be hired by the hour or day at most tourist centers, usually near the main station, and provide a convenient way to do sightseeing, cycle maps being provided.

この自動車／自転車の部品はありません。	I don't have parts for your car/bicycle
部品はどこか他へ取りに行かなければなりません。	I have to get the parts from somewhere else
部品を注文しなければなりません。	I have to order the parts
半日かかります。	That'll take half a day
一日かかります。	That'll take a day

二、三日かかります。	That'll take a few days
一週間かかります。	That'll take a week
全損です。	Your car is a write-off
全然修理出来ません。	It can't be repaired
…時に自動車／バイク／オートバイ／自転車を取りに来れます。	The car/motorcycle/moped/bicycle will be ready at ...o'clock

 Renting a vehicle

I'd like to rent a...	*... o karitigh-n des-nga* …を借りたいんですが。
Here is my driver's license	*Kore-ga watashi no unten-menkyo-sho des.* これが私の運転免許証です。
Do I need a (special) licence for that?	*(tokubets no) Unten menkyoshoh-ga irimas-ka* (特別の)運転免許証がいりますか。
I'd like to rent the... for...	*... kari-tigh-n-des-nga* …借りたいんですが。
– one day	*ichi-nichi* 一日
– two days	*futsuka* 二日
How much is that per day?	*Ichi-nichi ikura des-ka* 一日いくらですか？
– week?	*Is-shookan ikura des-ka* 一週間いくらですか？
How much is the deposit?	*Hoshoh-kin-wa ikura des-ka* 保証金はいくらですか？
Could I have a receipt for the deposit?	*Hoshoh-kin-no ryoh-shoo-sho o-negigh-shimas* 保証金の領収書お願いします。

The parts of a bicycle

(the diagram shows the numbered parts)

1	rear light	バック・ライト	*bakku right*
2	rear wheel	後車輪	*koh-sharin*
3	(luggage) carrier	荷台	*ni-digh*
4	bicycle fork	フォーク	*fohk*
5	bell	ベル	*beru*
	inner tube	チューブ	*choob*
	tire	タイヤ	*tigh-ya*
6	crank	クランク	*kurank*
7	gear change	変速機	*hen-soku-ki*
	wire	ワイヤー	*wigh-ya*
	generator	発電器	*hatsu-denki*
	frame	フレーム	*fraym*
8	dress guard	泥除け	*doro-yokay*
9	chain	チェーン	*chayn*
	chain guard	チェーン・カバー	*chayn kabah*
	odometer	走行距離計	*sohkoh kyohri-kay*
	child's seat	子供用いす	*kodomo-yoh isu*
10	headlight	ヘッドランプ	*heddo ramp*
	bulb	電球	*den-kyoo*
11	pedal	ペダル	*pedaru*
12	pump	空気入れ	*kooki-iray*
13	reflector	反射鏡	*hansha-kyoh*
14	brake shoe	ブレーキ・ブロック	*burayk-brok*
15	brake cable	ブレーキ・ケーブル	*burayk kayburu*
16	ring lock	キー	*kee*
17	carrier straps	荷台ロープ	*nidigh-rohp*
	tachometer	スピード・メーター	*speedo-mehtah*
18	spoke	スポーク	*spohk*
19	mudguard	泥よけ	*doro-yokay*
20	handlebar	ハンドル	*handoru*
21	chain wheel	チェーン・ホイール	*chayn hweeru*
	toe clip	トウクリップ	*toh-kuripp*
22	crank axle	クランク軸	*kurank-jiku*
	drum brake	ドラム・ブレーキ	*doram-burayk*
	rim	リム	*rimu*
23	valve	チューブ	*choob*
24	valve tube	タイヤバルブ	*tigh-ya barubu*
25	gear cable	ギア・ケーブル	*geeya kayburu*
26	fork	フォーク	*fohk*
27	front wheel	前車輪	*zen-sharin*
28	seat	サドル	*sadoru*

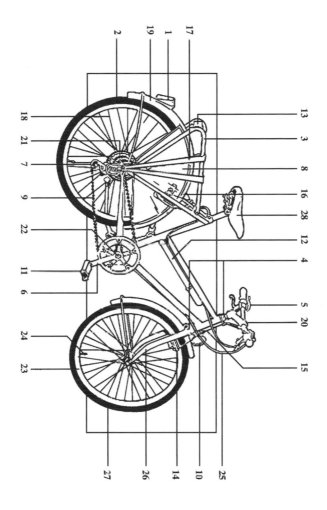

電動自転車
electric bicycle

How much is the surcharge per kilometer?	*Kirometoru-ni-tsuki tsuika-ryohkin-wa ikura des-ka* キロメートルにつき追加料金はいくらですか。
Does that include gas?	*Gasorin-digh-wa high-tay imas-ka* ガソリン代は入っていますか。
Does that include insurance?	*Hoken-wa fuku-maretay imas-ka* 保険は含まれていますか。
What time can I pick the...up tomorrow?	*Ashta nanji-ni tori-ni koremas-ka* 明日何時に取りにこれますか。
When does the...have to be back?	*Nanji maday-ni modoseba ee des-ka* 何時までに戻せばいいですか。
Where's the gas tank?	*Tank-wa doko des-ka* タンクはどこですか。
What sort of fuel does it take?	*Gasorin-wa nan-des-ka* ガソリンは何ですか。

5.7 Hitchhiking

Hitchhiking is rare in Japan, but foreign tourists sometimes do it.

Where are you heading?	*Doko-e ikimas-ka* どこへ行きますか。
Can I come along?	*Nosetay kudasa-e-mas-ka* 乗せて下さいますか。
Can my friend come too?	*Tomodachi-mo nosetay kudasa-e-mas-ka* 友達も乗せて下さいますか。
I'm trying to get to...	*... ni iki-tigh-n des-nga* …に行きたいんですが。
Is that on the way to...?	*... to onaji hoh-gaku des-ka* …と同じ方角ですか。
Could you drop me off...?	*... de oroshtay kuda-sigh* …で下ろして下さい。

– here?	*koko* ここ
– at the...exit?	*... no dequchi* …の出口
– in the center?	*chooshin* 中心
– at the next intersection?	*tsugi-no kohsaten* 次の交差点
Could you stop here, please?	*Koko-de tometay kuda-sigh* ここで止めて下さい。
I'd like to get out here	*Koko-de oroshtay kuda-sigh* ここで下ろして下さい。
Thanks for the lift	*Arigatoh goza-imashta* ありがとうございました。

6 Arrival and Departure

6. Arrival and Departure

6.1 General

Where does this train go to?	*Kono densha-wa doko-e ikimas-ka* この電車はどこへ行きますか。
Does this boat go to...?	*Kono funay-wa ... e ikimas-ka* この船は…へ行きますか。
Can I take this bus to...?	*Kono bas-wa ... e ikimas-ka* このバスは…へ行きますか。
Does this train stop at...?	*Kono densha-wa ... ni tomarimas-ka* この電車は…に止まりますか。
Are these the priority seats?	*Kono seki-wa you-sen seki des-ka* この席は優先席ですか。
Is this seat free?	*Kono seki-wa ightay imas-ka* この席は空いていますか。
– reserved?	*Kore-wa shtay-seki des-ka* これは指定席ですか。
I've reserved...	*Yoyaku shimashta* 予約しました
Could you tell me where I have to get off for... ?	*... e iku-ni-wa, doko-de oriru-ka oshi-etay kuda-sigh* …へ行くには、どこで降りるか教えてください。
Could you let me know when we get to...?	*... ni tsui-tara oshi-etay kuda-sigh* …に着いたら教えて下さい。
Could you stop at the next stop, please?	*Tsugi-no bas-tay-de oroshtay kuda-sigh* 次のバス停で下ろして下さい。
Where are we now?	*Ima dono-hen des-ka* 今どのへんですか。
Do I have to get off here?	*Koko-de ori-nakereba-narimasen-ka* ここで降りなければなりませんか。
Have we already passed...?	*Moh ... o tohri-mashta-ka* もう…を通りましたか。

How long have I been asleep?	*Watasi-wa dono gurigh nemuri-mashta-ka* 私はどのぐらい眠りましたか。
How long does...stop here?	*... wa koko-ni dono-kurigh tomattay imas-ka* …はここにどのくらい止まっていますか。
I have Japan Rail Pass	*JR pas wo motte imas* JRパス を持っています。
Can I come back on the same ticket?	*Kono kippu-wa ohf-ku des-ka* この切符は往復ですか。
Can I change on this ticket?	*Kono kippu-de norikae-raremas-ka* この切符で乗り換えられますか。
How long is this ticket valid for?	*Kono kippu-wa itsu maday yookoh des-ka* この切符はいつまで有効ですか。

6.2 Customs

A passport is necessary for all visitors to Japan. Citizens of most European countries do not need a visa if they are staying as tourists up to 90 days. Visitors from the US, Canada, and New Zealand need a visa for visits of over 90 days. They are easily obtainable and free. Visitors from Australia need a visa for any visit. Drugs, firearms, and pornography may not be taken into Japan. Non-residents can take in duty-free 400 cigarettes, or 100 cigars, or 500g of tobacco; 3 bottles of alcohol (760cc each); 50g perfume; and other goods up to 200,000 yen in value. Personal possessions are exempt.

パスポートを見せて下さい。	Your passport, please
ビザを見せて下さい。	Your visa, please
どこへ行きますか。	Where are you heading?

どのくらい滞在しますか。	How long are you planning to stay?
申告する品はありますか。	Do you have anything to declare?
これを開けて見せて下さい。	Open this, please

I'm going on vacation to...   *Kyooka-de ... e ikimas*
休暇で…へ行きます。

I'm on a business trip   *Shutchoh des*
出張です。

I don't know how long   *Dono-gurigh tigh-zai suru-ka mada*
I'll be staying yet   *wakarimasen*
どのぐらい滞在するかまだ分かりません。

I'll be staying here   *Kono shoo-mats dakay imas*
for a weekend   この週末だけいます。

– for a few days   *Ni, san-nichi imas*
二、三日います。

– for a week   *I-shookan imas*
一週間います。

– for two weeks   *Ni-shookan imas*
二週間います。

I've got nothing   *Nani-mo shinkoku suru mono-wa*
to declare   *arimasen*
何も申告する物はありません。

I've got...with me   *... o mottay imas*
…を持っています。

...100 cigarettes   *Tabako-wa hyappon arimas*
たばこは百本あります。

– ...1 bottle of...   *... wa ippon arimas*
…は一本あります。

– some souvenirs   *Omlyagay-nga sukoshi arimas*
おみやげが少しあります。

These are personal   *Koray-wa jibun-de tsukau mono des*
possessions   これは自分で使う物です。

These are not new   *Koray-wa ata-rashiku arimasen*
これは新しくありません。

Here's the receipt	*Ryohshoo-sho des* 領収書です。
How much import tax do I have to pay?	*Yunyoo-zay-wa ikura des-ka* 輸入税はいくらですか。
Can I go now?	*Ittay-mo ee des-ka* 行ってもいいですか。

6.3 Luggage

Porter!	*Pohtah-san* ポーターさん！
Could you take this luggage to...?	*Kono nimots-o ... ni mottay ittay kuda-sigh* この荷物を…に持って行って下さい。
How much do I owe you?	*Ikura des-ka* いくらですか。
Where can I find a luggage cart?	*Dighsha-wa doko-ni arimas-ka* 台車はどこにありますか。
Could you store this luggage for me?	*Kono nimots-o azukattay mo-rae-mas-ka* この荷物を預かってもらえますか。
Where are the luggage lockers?	*Rokkah-wa doko des-ka* ロッカーはどこですか。
I can't get the locker open	*Rokkah-ga akimasen* ロッカーが空きません。
How much is it per item per day?	*Ichinichi ikko ikura des-ka* 一日一個いくらですか。
This is not my bag/ suitcase	*Watashi-no kaban de wa arimasen* 私のカバンではありません。
There's one bag/ suitcase missing still	*Kaban-ga hitots tarimasen* カバンが一つ足りません。
My suitcase is damaged	*Kaban-ga kowarete-imasu* カバンが壊れています。

6.4 Questions to passengers

Ticket types

Eチケット	e-ticket
この切符は…ですか。	Is this ticket...?
一等	first class
二等	second class
片道	one-way
往復	round-trip
喫煙車	smoking
禁煙車	no-smoking
窓側の座席	window
通路側の座席	aisle
列車の前方	front
列車の後方	back
座席	seat
寝台車	berth
上・中・下	top, middle or bottom
エコノミークラスあるいはビジネスクラス？	Tourist class or business class?
室あるいは座席？	Cabin or seat?
一人用あるいは二人用？	Single or double?
何人ですか。	How many are travelling?

Destination

どこへ行きますか。	Where are you travelling to?
いつ出発しますか。	When are you leaving?
…に出発します。	Your... leaves at...
乗り換えなければなりません。	You have to change trains
…で降りなければなりません。	You have to get off at...
…経由で行かなければなりません。	You have to travel via...
出発は…です。	The outward journey is on...

帰りは…です。	The return journey is on...
…までに乗船しなければなりません。	You have to be on board by....

Inside the vehicle

切符を見せて下さい。	Your ticket, please
指定席券を見せて下さい。	Your reservation, please
パスポートを見せて下さい。	Your passport, please
座席が違います。	You're in the wrong seat
違った…ですが。	You're on/in the wrong...
これは指定席です。	This seat is reserved
特別料金を払わなければなりません。	You'll have to pay an extra fare
…は…分遅れています。	The...has been delayed by... minutes

6.5 Tickets

Where can I buy a ticket?	*Kippu-wa doko-de ka-emas-ka* 切符はどこで買えますか。
– make a reservation?	*Doko-de yoyaku dekimas-ka* どこで予約出来ますか。
– reserve a flight?	*Shikohki-no kippu-wa doko-de ka-emas-ka* 飛行機の切符はどこで買えますか。
Could I have a one-way, please?	*Katamichi onegigh-shimas* 片道お願いします。
– a round-trip?	*Ohfuku onegigh-shimas* 往復お願いします。
first class	*ittoh-sha* 一等車

second class	*nitoh-sha* 二等車
tourist class	*ekonomi-kurasu* エコノミークラス
business class	*bijines-kuras* ビジネスクラス
I'd like to reserve a seat	*Zaseki-o yoyaku shitigh-n des* 座席を予約したいんです。
– berth	*Shin-digh-sha-o yoyaku shitigh-n-des* 寝台車を予約したいんです。
– aisle seats	*tsu-ro gawa no seki* 通路側の席
top/middle/bottom	*weh/naka/shta* 上／中／下
I'd like to reserve a cabin	*Senshits-o yoyaku shitigh-n des* 船室を予約したいんです。
smoking/no smoking	*kitsu-en/kin(g)-en* 喫煙／禁煙
by the window	*mado-giwa-de* 窓際で
single/double	*shtori-yoh/f-tari-yoh* 一人用／二人用
at the front/back of the train	*ressha-no zempoh-de/ressha-no koh-hoh-de* 列車の前方で／列車の後方で
– of the plane	*sh-kohki-no zempoh-de/sh-kohki-no koh-hoh-de* 飛行機の前方で／飛行機の後方で
One car	*Kuruma-wa ichi-digh des* 車は一台です。
... bicycles	*Jitensha-wa ...digh des* 自転車は…台です。
Do you also have season tickets?	*Tayki-ken-mo arimas-ka* 定期券もありますか。

Arrival and Departure

6

Where's...?	*... wa doko des-ka* …はどこですか。
Where's the information desk?	*An-nigh-jo-wa doko des-ka* 案内所はどこですか。
Where can I find a schedule?	*Jikoku-hyoh-wa doko des-ka* 時刻表はどこですか。
Where's the...desk?	*... no uriba-wa doko des-ka* …の売場はどこですか。
Do you have a city map with the bus/the subway routes on it?	*Bas-ya chika-tets-ga nottay iru machi-no chizu-wa arimas-ka* バスや地下鉄が載っている町の地図 はありますか。
Do you have a schedule?	*Jikoku-hyoh arimas-ka* 時刻表ありますか。
I'd like to confirm my reservation for/trip to...	*... maday-no ryokoh/yoyaku-o tashi-kametay oki-tigh-n des* …までの旅行／予約を確かめておき たいんです。
I'd like to cancel my reservation for/trip to...	*... maday-no ryokoh/yoyaku-o torikeshi-tigh-n des* …までの旅行／予約を取り消したい んです。
I'd like to change my reservation for/trip to...	*... maday-no ryokoh/yoyaku-o ka-e-tigh-n des* …までの旅行／予約を変えたいんです。
Will I get my money back?	*Ha-righ modoshi-o saykyoo dekimas-ka* 払戻しを請求出来ますか。
I want to go to... How do I get there? (What's the quickest way there?)	*... e iki-tigh-n des-nga, dono-yoh-ni ikimas-ka (nani-ga ichiban ha-yigh des-ka)* …へ行きたいんですが、どのように行 きますか（何が一番速いですか）。

Do I have to pay extra?	*Tswee-ka ryohkin-o harawa-nakereba-narimasen-ka* 追加料金を払わなければなりませんか。
How much is a single to...?	*... maday-no katamichi-wa ikura des-ka* …までの片道はいくらですか。
How much is a return to...?	*... maday-no ohf-ku-wa ikura des-ka* …までの往復はいくらですか。
Can I interrupt my journey with this ticket?	*Kono kippu-de tochoo gesha-ga dekimas-ka* この切符で途中下車が出来ますか。
How much luggage am I allowed?	*Nimots-wa nankiro-maday mottay ikemas-ka* 荷物は何キロまで持って行けますか。
Can I send my luggage in advance?	*Nimots-o takkyoo-bin-de okuremas-ka* 荷物を宅急便で送れますか。
Does this...travel direct?	*Kono ... wa chokkoh des-ka* この…は直行ですか。
Do I have to change? Where?	*Norikae-nakereba-narimasen-ka, doko-de* 乗り換えなければなりませんか。どこで
Will there be any stopovers?	*Tochoo tomarimas-ka* 途中止まりますか。
Does the boat call at any ports on the way?	*Tochoo minato-ni kikoh shimas-ka* 途中港に寄港しますか。
Does the train/bus stop at...?	*Kono densha (bas)-wa ... ni tomarimas-ka* この電車（バス）は…に止まりますか。
Where should I get off?	*Doko-de ori-nakereba-narimasen ka* どこで降りなければなりませんか。
Is there a connection to...?	*... maday-no setsu-zoku-wa arimas-ka* …までの接続はありますか。
How long do I have to wait?	*Dono gurigh mata-nakereba-narimasen-ka* どのぐらい待たなければなりませんか。

When does...leave?	*... wa its shuppats shimas-ka* …はいつ出発しますか。
What time does the next...leave?	*Tsugi-no ....wa nanji-ni shuppats shimas-ka* 次の…は何時に出発しますか。
What time does the last...leave?	*Sigh-shoo-no ... wa nanji-ni shuppats shimas-ka* 最終の…は何時に出発しますか。
How long does...take?	*Dono-gurigh kakarimas-ka* どのぐらいかかりますか。
What time does... arrive in...?	*... ni nanji-ni tsukimas-ka* …に何時に着きますか。
Where does the...to... leave from?	*... maday-no densha-wa doko-kara shuppats shimas-ka* …までの電車はどこから出発しますか。
Is this the train/bus/ boat to...?	*Koray-wa ... maday-no densha/bas/ funay des-ka* これは…までの電車／バス／船ですか。

6.7 Airports

到着 arrivals	インターネットラウンジ Internet lounge	空港内ホテル airport hotels
出発 departures	空港警備／ 　空港セキュリティー airport security	手荷物受取所 baggage claim
国際 international	E-ブッキング e-booking/reservations	セキュリティー security
国内 domestic		金属探知機 metal detector
スキャナー scanner	チェックイン checking in	ペースメーカー pacemaker
搭乗券 boarding pass	手荷物引換券 baggage claim check	

 **Trains**

● **The railway system in Japan is very well developed**, and managed by Japan Railways (JR) and a large number of private railway companies. Intercity trains are local (*futsoo*), express (*kyoo-koh*), limited express (*tokkyoo*), and super express (*shinkansen*).

Tickets are charged by distance, with surcharges for the category of train, class, and seat reservations. Ticket reservations are made at counters called "green windows" (*midori no madoguchi*). Tickets can be bought from ticket machines and most of these have an English option. The full fare does not have to be paid before the destination. Fare adjustment machines and counters are available. All JR stations show station names written in Japanese with the romanization below. Useful for travelers is the custom of including the names of the previous and next stations to the left and right underneath the station name.

 **Taxis**

● **Taxis are expensive, but all are metered and there is no custom of tipping.** Carry the address and phone number of your destination, and a map of the immediate location if possible, to give to the driver. Taxi doors are automated; normally the back curbside door is the only one used. On arrival, wait for the driver to open the door, and do not close it yourself.

空車	満車	タクシー乗り場
for hire	booked	taxi stand

Taxi	*Tak-shee* タクシー！	
Could you get me a taxi, please?	*Tak-shee-o yonday kuda-sigh* タクシーを呼んで下さい。	
Where can I find a taxi around here?	*Tak-shee noriba-wa doko des-ka* タクシー乗り場はどこですか。	

Could you take me to..., please?	*... maday o-negigh shimas* …までお願いします。
– this address	*kono joosho* この住所
– the...hotel	*... hoteru* …ホテル
– the town/city center	*choo-shin-chi* 中心地
– the station	*eki* 駅
– the airport	*koo-koh* 空港
How much is the trip to...?	*... maday ikura des-ka* …までいくらですか。
How far is it to...?	*... maday nan-kiro gurigh des-ka* …まで何キロぐらいですか。
I'm in a hurry	*Iso-iday irun des-nga* 急いでいるんですが
Could you speed up/ slow down a little?	*Motto hayaku/yukkuri ittay kuda-sigh* もっと速く／ゆっくり行ってください。
Could you take a different route?	*Hoka-no michi-o tottay kuda-sigh* 他の道を取って下さい。
I'd like to get out here, please	*Koko-de oroshtay kuda-sigh* ここで下ろして下さい。
You have to go straight on	*... massugu ittay kuda-sigh* …真っ直ぐ行ってください。
You have to turn left	*... hidari-ni magattay kuda-sigh* …左に曲がって下さい。
You have to turn right	*... migi-ni magattay kuda-sigh* …右に曲がって下さい。
This is it	*Koko des* ここです。
Could you wait a minute for me, please?	*Chotto mattay-tay kuda-sigh* ちょっと待ってて下さい。

7 A Place to Stay

7. A Place to Stay

● **Japan has a great variety of overnight accommodation.**
There is a wide range of hotels, from five-star international
hotels to business hotels and small local establishments. The
cheaper the hotel, the smaller the room and the fewer the facilities. Whatever the grade of hotel, cleanliness should be of high
order. Other accommodation, especially in country areas, includes
the very expensive luxury *ryokan* (traditional inns) and small,
cheaper inns. Inns are a good way to experience the Japanese life-
style. Rooms are covered with straw mats (*tatami*) and the guest
sleeps on a mattress (*futon*) spread on the floor. In some inns
meals (Japanese style) are also served in the room. Bathing is
generally communal (men's and women's facilities are separated)
in a large room containing a sunken bath (very hot) for relaxa-
tion and individual taps and stools to wash prior to entering the
bath. In rural areas these baths may be *onsen* (hot springs).

Many small inns now operate as *minshuku*, inexpensive accommodation offering two meals. These can be booked through the
travel counters at stations and airports, or through the Internet.
They are a good option especially when travelling in the country.
In the last few years a western version called *pension* has also
become popular. Camping is not popular, and campsites are few
and poor in the way of facilities. Youth hostels, of which there is
an extensive network, provide a cheap alternative.

いつまでお泊まりですか。	How long will you be staying?
この用紙に記入して下さい。	Fill in this form, please
パスポートをお願いします。	Could I see your passport?
保証金をお願いします。	I'll need a deposit
前払いでお願いします。	You'll have to pay in advance

My name's...I've made a reservation...	*Watashi-wa ... des. heya-no yoyaku-o shtay arimas* 私は…です。部屋の予約をしてあります。
– over the phone	*denwa-de* 電話で
– by mail	*tegami-de* 手紙で
– by email	*may-ru de* メールで
How much is it per night/week/ month?	*Ippaku/isshookan/ikkagets-wa ikura des-ka* 一泊／一週間／一ヶ月はいくらですか。
We'll be staying at least two nights/two weeks	*Semetay nihaku/nishookan tomari-tigh-n-des-nga* せめて二泊／二週間泊まりたいんですが。
We don't know yet	*Mada wakarimasen-nga* まだ分かりませんが。
What time does the gate/door open?	*Nanji-ni akimas-ka* 何時に開きますか。
– close?	*Nanji-ni shimarimas-ka* 何時に閉まりますか。
Could you get me a taxi, please?	*Takshee-o yonday kuremasen-ka* タクシーを呼んでくれませんか。
Is there any message left for me?	*Watashi-atay-no messe-ji/dengon-ga arimas-ka* 私宛のメッセージ・伝言がありますか。

A Place to Stay

7.2 Hotels/B&Bs/apartments/holiday rentals

Do you have a single available?	*Shtori-beya arimas-ka* 一人部屋ありますか。
– double room...	*Ftari-beya arimas-ka* 二人部屋ありますか。

per person/per room	*shtori-ni-tski/ hito-heya-ni-tski* 一人に付き／一部屋に付き
Does that include breakfast/lunch/dinner?	*Choh-shoku/choo-shoku/yoo-shoku tski-mas-ka* 朝食／昼食／夕食付きですか。
Could we have two adjoining rooms?	*Tonari-awase-no heya arimas-ka* 隣り合わせの部屋ありますか。
with toilet/bath/shower	*toyray/bas/shawah-tski-no heya* トイレ／バス／シャワー付きの部屋
without toilet/bath/ shower	*toyray/bas/shawah-nashi-no heya* トイレ／バス／シャワーなしの部屋
facing the street	*michi-ni men-shtay iru heya* 道に面している部屋
not facing the street	*michi-ni men-shtay i-nigh heya* 道に面していない部屋
with a view of the sea	*umi-gawa-no heya* 海側の部屋
without a view of the sea	*umi-ni men-shtay i-nigh heya* 海に面していない部屋
Is there an elevator in the hotel?	*Erebehtah arimas-ka* エレベーターありますか。
Do you have room service?	*Room-sahbis arimas-ka* ルームサービスありますか。
self-catering accommodation	*sudomari* 素泊まり
Could I see the room?	*Heya-o misetay moraemas-ka* 部屋を見せてもらえますか。
I'll take this room	*Kono-heya-ni kime-mashta* この部屋に決めました。
Please show us another room	*Hoka-no heya-o misetay kuda-sigh* 他の部屋を見せて下さい。
Do you have a larger room?	*Motto ohkee heya-wa arimasen-ka* もっと大きい部屋はありませんか。
Do you have a less expensive room?	*Motto yasui heya-wa arimasen-ka* もっと安い部屋はありませんか。

| Could you put in a cot? | *Kodomo-yoh-no beddo-o tsweeka-dekimas-ka*
子供用のベッドを追加できますか。 |
| What time's breakfast? | *Choh-shoku-wa nanji des-ka*
朝食は何時ですか。 |

トイレやバスは同階／ 　部屋にあります。	You can find the toilet and shower 　on the same floor/in the room
トイレやバスは部屋 　にあります。	The toilet and shower are in 　your room
こちらです。	This way, please
…階にあります。	Your room is on the...floor
部屋番号は…番です。	Your room is number...

Where's the dining room?	*Shokudoh-wa doko des-ka* 食堂はどこですか。
Can I have breakfast in my room?	*Choh-shoku-o heya-de tabe-rare-mas-ka* 朝食を部屋で食べられますか。
Where's the emergency exit?	*Hijoh-guchi-wa doko des-ka* 非常口はどこですか。
– fire escape?	*Hijoh kigh-dan-wa doko des-ka* 非常階段はどこですか。
Where can I park my car?	*Doko-ni choo-sha dekimas-ka* どこに駐車出来ますか。
The key to room..., please	*...ban-no heya-no kagi o-negigh-shimas* …番の部屋の鍵お願いします。
Could you put this in the safe, please?	*Koray-o kinko-ni iretay kuda-sigh-mas-ka* これを金庫に入れて下さいますか。
Could you wake me at...tomorrow?	*Ashta ...ji-ni okoshtay kuda-sigh* 明日…時に起こして下さい。
Could you find a babysitter for me?	*Bebee-shitta-ga hoshee-n des-nga* ベビーシッターがほしいんですが。

Could I have an extra blanket?	*Sumimasen-nga, mohfu moh ichi-migh o-negigh-shimas* すみませんが、毛布もう一枚お願いします。
What days do the cleaners come in?	*Osohji-wa nanyohbi des-ka* お掃除は何曜日ですか。
When are the sheets/ towels changed?	*Its sheets/taoru-o tori-ka-emas-ka* いつシーツ／タオルを取り替えますか。

 Complaints

We can't sleep for the noise	*Uru-sakutay nemure-nigh-n-des* うるさくて眠れないんです。
Could you turn the radio down, please?	*Rajio-no onryo-o sagetay kuda-sigh* ラジオの音量を下げて下さい。
We're out of toilet paper	*Toyretto-pehpah-ga naigh-n-des-nga* トイレットペーパーがないんですが。
There aren't any.../ there's not enough...	*... ga tari-nigh-n-des* …が足りないんです。
The bed linen's dirty	*Sheets-ga kita-nigh-no-des-nga* シーツがきたないのですが。
The room hasn't been cleaned	*Heya-ga sohji shtay arimasen* 部屋が掃除してありません。
The heater's not working	*Damboh-ga kii-te imasen* 暖房がきいていません。
The air conditioning's not working	*E-a-kon-ga kii-te imasen* エアコンがきいていません。
There's no water	*Mizu-ga demasen* 水が出ません。
– hot water	*Oyu-ga demasen* お湯が出ません。
– electricity	*Denki-ga arimasen* 電気がありません。
...is broken	*... ga kowaretay imas* …がこわれています。

Could you have that seen to?	*Sono-yoh-ni yoroshku o-negigh-shimas* そのようによろしくお願いします。
Could I have another room/site?	*Hoka-no heya-ni ka-etay kuda-sigh* 他の部屋に替えて下さい。
The bed creaks terribly	*Beddo-ga sugoi oto-o tateru-n-des-nga* ベッドがすごい音をたてるんですが。
The bed sags	*Beddo-ga yawaraka-sugimas* ベッドが柔らか過ぎます。
There are bugs/insects in our room	*Heya-ni mushi-ga iru-n-des-nga* 部屋に虫がいるんですが。
This place is full of...	*Koko-ni-wa ... ga takusan itay, komarimas* ここには…がたくさんいて、こまります。
– mosquitos	*ka* 蚊
– cockroaches	*go-kiburi* ゴキブリ

 **7.4** **Departure**

See also 8.2 Settling the bill

I'm leaving tomorrow. Could I pay my bill, please?	*Ashta tachi-mas-kara saysan shtay kuda-sigh* 明日立ちますから、精算して下さい。
What time should we check out?	*Nanji maday-ni heya-o ake nakereba-narimasen-ka* 何時までに部屋をあけなければなりませんか。
Could I have my deposit/passport back, please?	*Hoshoh-kln/paspohto-o kigh shtay kuda-sigh* 保証金／パスポートを返して下さい。
Could you forward my mail to this address?	*Kono joosho-ni tegami-o tensoh shtay kuda-sigh-mas-ka* この住所に手紙を転送して下さいますか。

We're in a terrible hurry	*Tigh-hen isoi-de imas* 大変急いでいます。
Could we leave our luggage here until we leave?	*Shuppats-maday nimots-o koko-ni oitay itay-mo ee des-ka* 出発まで荷物をここに置いていてもいいですか。
Thanks for your hospitality	*Omotenashi arigatoh go-zigh-mashta* おもてなしありがとうございました。

7.5 Camping

See the diagram on page 99

ご自分で場所を決めて下さい。	You can pick your own site
場所が割り当てられています。	You'll be allocated a site
あなたの場所の番号です。	This is your site number
自動車に貼り付けて下さい。	Stick this on your car, please

Where's the manager?	*Kanri-nin-wa doko des-ka* 管理人はどこですか。
Are we allowed to camp here?	*Koko-de kyamp dekimas-ka* ここでキャンプ出来ますか。
Can we pick our own site?	*Jibun-de basho-o kimetay-mo ee des-ka* 自分で場所を決めてもいいですか。
Do you have a quiet spot for us?	*Shizuka-na basho-ga arimas-ka* 静かな場所がありますか。
Do you have any other sites available?	*Hoka-ni basho-ga arimasen-ka* 他に場所がありませんか。
It's too windy/sunny/here	*Koko-wa kazay/hizashi-ga tsuyo-sugi-mas* ここは風／日ざしが強過ぎます。
It's too crowded here	*Koko-wa komi-sugi-tay mas* ここは混み過ぎています。

The ground's too hard/uneven	*Jimen-wa kata-sugimas/deko-boko des* 地面は堅過ぎます／でこぼこです
Do you have a level spot for the camper/trailer/folding trailer?	*Kyamping-kah-no tamay-ni tighra-na basho-ga arimas-ka* キャンピングカーのために平らな場所がありますか。
Could we have adjoining sites?	*Issho-ni tate-rareru basho-ga arimas-ka* 一緒に立てられる場所がありますか。
Can we park the car next to the tent?	*Tento-no tonari-ni choosha shtay-mo ee des-ka* テントの隣に駐車してもいいですか。
How much is it per person/tent/trailer/car?	*Shtori/tento ikko/kyamping-kah ichi-digh/kuruma ichi-digh-wa ikura des-ka* 一人／テント一個／キャンピングカー一台／車一台はいくらですか。
Do you have any huts to rent?	*Kashi-goya-mo arimas-ka* 貸小屋もありますか。
Are there any...?	*... arimas-ka* …ありますか。
– hot showers?	*oyu-no shawah* お湯のシャワー…
– washing machines?	*sentakki* 洗濯機
Is there a children's play area on the site?	*Kyamp-jo-ni-wa kodomoyoh-no asobiba-ga arimas-ka* キャンプ場には、子供用の遊び場がありますか。
Can I rent a locker here?	*Rokkah-ga kari-raremas-ka* ロッカーが借りられますか。
Are there any power outlets?	*Denki-o tsuka-emas-ka* 電気を使えますか。
Is there drinking water?	*Nomi-mizu wa arimas-ka* 飲み水はありますか。
When's the garbage collected?	*Gomi-wa its atsume-mas-ka* ごみはいつ集めますか。

Camping equipment

(the diagram shows the numbered parts)

	luggage space	荷物置場	nimots-okiba
	can opener	かん切り	kan-kiri
	butane gas bottle	ブタン・ガスボンベ	butan-gas-bombay
1	tool bag	自転車用バッグ	jitensha-yoh baggu
2	gas cooker	ガス・コンロ	gas-konro
3	groundsheet	グランドシート	gurando sheeto
	hammer	かなずち	kana-zuchi
	hammock	ハンモック	hammok
4	gas can	燃料タンク	nenryoh-tank
	campfire	キャンプファイヤー	kyamp figh-ya
5	folding chair	折りたたみ式キャンプ用いす	oritatami-shki kyamp-yoh isu
6	insulated picnic box	クール・ボックス	kooru bokks
	ice pack	アイスパック	ighs-pakku
	compass	コンパス	kompas
	wick	芯	shin
	corkscrew	コルク栓抜き	kork-sen-nuki
7	airbed	エア・マットレス	e-a mattres
8	airbed plug	プラグ	prag
	pump	空気入れ	kooki iray
9	awning	日よけ	hi-yokay
10	mat	マットレス	mattres
11	pan	鍋	nabay
12	pan handle	鍋つかみ	nabay ts-kami
	primus stove	コンロ	konro
	zip	ファスナー／ジッパー	fasnah/jippah
13	backpack	リュックサック	ryuk-sakk
14	guy rope	張り網	hari-zuna
	sleeping bag	寝袋	ne-bukuro
15	storm lantern	ランタン／灯油ランプ	rantan/toh-yoo ramp
	camp bed	キャンプ用ベッド	kyamp-yoh beddo
	table	折りたたみ式（キャンプ用）テーブル	oritatami-shki (kyamp-yoh) tayburu
16	tent	テント	tento
17	tent peg	ペグ	pegg
18	tent pole	テント・ポール	tento-pohru
	thermos	魔法瓶	mahohbin
19	water bottle	水筒	sweetoh
	clothes hook	洗濯バサミ	sentaku-basami
	clothes line	物干しロープ	monohoshi rohp
	windbreak	風よけ	kaze-yoke
20	flashlight	懐中電灯／ポケットライト	kigh-choo den-toh/pokett-righ-to
	pocket knife	小刀	kogatana

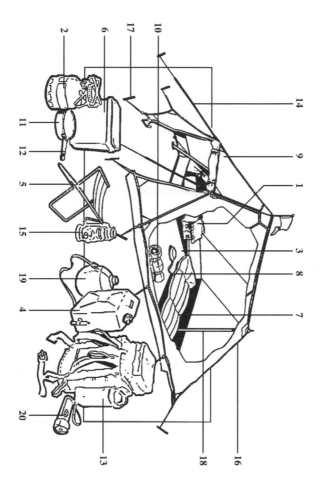

8 Money Matters

8. Money Matters

● In general, banks are open Monday–Friday 9–3. They are closed on Saturdays, Sundays, and national holidays. Travelers' checks in yen or dollars are easily cashed at banks, but they are not readily acceptable outside the hotels and shops that cater particularly for the international traveler. Cash can be obtained from cash machines at selected convenience stores in city areas.

 ## 8.1 Banks

Where can I find a bank/ an exchange office around here?	*Kono-hen-ni ginkoh-wa arimas-ka* この辺に銀行はありますか。
Where can I find a post office around here?	*Kono-hen-ni yoobin-kyoku-wa arimas-ka* この辺に郵便局はありますか。
Where can I cash this traveler's check/giro check?	*kono (ryokoh-yoh) kogit-tay-wa doko-de genkin-ni ka-eraremas-ka* この（旅行用）小切手はどこで現金に替えられますか。
Can I cash this...here?	*Kono ... wa koko-de genkin-ni ka-eraremas-ka* この…はここで現金に替えられますか。
I'd like to withdraw cash	*Okane-o oroshi-tigh no des-ga* お金をおろしたいのですが。
Can I withdraw money on my credit card here?	*Krejitto-kahdo-de genkin-o hiki-dasemas-ka* クレジットカードで現金を引き出せますか。
What's the minimum/ maximum amount?	*Sigh-shoh/sigh-koh-wa ikura des-ka* 最小／最高はいくらですか。
Can I take out less than that?	*Skoshi-demo ee des-ka* 少しでもいいですか。

This is my bank/giro number	*Koray-wa watashi-no kohza bango des* これは私の口座番号です。
I've had some money transferred here. Has it arrived yet? These are the details of my bank in the U.S.	*Koko-ni o-kanay-o sohkin shtay morigh-mashta-nga, moh nyookin saretay imas-ka. koray-wa Amerika-no ginkoh no shoh-sho des* ここにお金を送金してもらいましたが、もう入金されていますか。これはアメリカの銀行の証書です。
What's the exchange rate?	*Kawasay rayto-wa ikura des-ka* 為替レートはいくらですか。
I'd like to change some money	*Okanay-o ryoh-gae shtigh-n des-nga* お金を両替したいんですが。
– pounds into yen	*pondo-o yen-ni* ポンドを円に
– dollars into yen	*doru-o yen-ni* ドルを円に
Could you give me some small change with it?	*Komakigh okanay-mo iretay kuda-sigh* こまかいお金も入れて下さい。
This is not right	*Machigattay iru-to omoimas-nga* 間違っていると思いますが

ここに署名して下さい。	Sign here, please
これに記入して下さい。	Fill this out, please
パスポートを見せて下さい。	Could I see your passport, please?
身分証明書を見せて下さい。	Could I see some identification, please?
バンクカード／キャッシュカードを見せて下さい。	Could I see your bank/cashcard, please?

8.2 Settling the bill

| Could you put it on my bill? | *Heya-ni tsketay oitay kuda-sigh*
部屋に付けておいてください。 |

Does this amount include the tip?	*Sahbis-ryoh-wa hight-tay imas-ka* サービス料は入っていますか。
Can I pay by...?	*... de harae-mas-ka* …で払えますか。
– credit card?	*krejitto-kahdo* クレジットカード
– traveler's check?	*ryokoh-yoh kogit-tay* 旅行用小切手
You've given me too much	*Otsuri-ga oh-sugimas* おつりが多すぎます。
You haven't given me enough change	*Otsuri-ga sku-nigh des-nga* おつりが少ないのですが。
Could you check this again, please?	*Moh ichido tashi-kametay kuda-sigh-masen-ka* もう一度確かめてくださいませんか。
Could I have a receipt, please?	*Ryoh-shoo-sho o-negigh-shimas* 領収書お願いします。
I don't have enough money on me	*Sumimasen-nga, mochi-ganay-nga tarimasen* すみませんが、持ち金が足りません。

クレジットカード／旅行用小切手／
外貨はご使用になれません。

We don't accept credit
cards/traveler's checks/
foreign currency

This is for you	*Dohzo* どうぞ。
Keep the change	*Otsuri-wa tottay oitay kuda-sigh* お釣りはとっておいてください。
Please enter your PIN number	*Ansho-bango wo new-ryoku shite kuda-sigh* 暗証番号を入力してください。

9 Mail, Phone and Internet

9. Mail, Phone and Internet

 Mail

● **Post offices open 9–5 Monday-Friday,** with cash-related facilities available until 3pm. The main offices in each ward are also open on Saturday mornings, 9–12:30. They are closed on Sundays and national holidays. However, they have after-hours services available for designated items, such as foreign mail. You must press the buzzer near the entrance and an attendant will come out to you. The Central Post Office across from Tokyo Station is open 24 hours a day. You can address letters using the English script (*romaji*).

郵便為替 money orders	郵便小包み parcels	電報 telegrams	切手 stamps

Where's the post office/ main post office?	*Kono-hen-ni yoo-bin-kyoku (yoo-bin-kyoku-no hon-kyoku)-wa arimas-ka* この辺に郵便局(郵便局の本局)はありますか。
Where's the mailbox?	*Kono-hen-ni posto-wa arimas-ka* この辺にポストはありますか。
Which counter should I go to...?	*... wa dono mado-guchi des-ka* …はどの窓口ですか。
– to send a fax	*fakks* ファックス
– to change money	*genkln ats-kigh* 現金扱い
– to change giro checks	*kogitay* 小切手
– for a Telegraph Money Order?	*denshin kawasay* 電信為替

Is there any mail for me? My name's...	*Watashi-atay-no yoobin-wa arimas-ka. watashi-no na-migh-wa ... des* 私宛の郵便はありますか。私の名前は…です。

Stamps

What's the postage for a letter to...?	*... made-no tegami-wa ikura des-ka* …までの手紙はいくらですか。
What's the postage for a postcard to...?	*... made-no hagaki-wa ikura des-ka* …までの葉書はいくらですか。
Are there enough stamps on it?	*Kittay-wa tarimas-ka* 切手は足りますか。
I'd like... ...yen stamps	*...yen-no kittay-o ...migh onegigh-shimas* …円の切手を…枚お願いします。
I'd like to send this express.	*Kore-o sokutats-bin-de o-negigh-shimas* これを速達便でお願いします。
– by air mail	*Kore-o kohkoobin-de o-negigh-shimas* これを航空便でお願いします。
– by registered mail	*Kore-o kaki-tomay-de o-negigh-shimas* これを書留でお願いします。

Fax/scan

Shall I fill out the form myself?	*Yohshi-wa jibun-de kinyoo shimashoh-ka* 用紙は自分で記入しましょうか。
Can I make photocopies here?	*Koko-de kopee dekimas-ka* ここでコピー出来ますか。
– send a fax here?	*Koko-de fakks dekimas-ka* ここでファックス出来ますか。
How much is it per page?	*Ippayji-wa ikura des-ka* 一ページはいくらですか。
Can I scan this here?	*Kore-wo scan she-tigh no des-ga* これをスキャンしたいのですが。

9.2 Telephone

● **Dialing procedures are shown** by diagrams inside phone boxes. Direct international calls can be made from card phones, most green phones, and some grey ones. If a phone can be used to dial abroad, the phone box will display a message in English to this effect. However, owing to the abuse of telephone cards for international calls, it may not be possible to use some card phones to dial overseas. The basic unit-cost is 10 yen per minute. Fax machines are widely available.

International calls can also be made via a telephone company (eg. NTT) using credit cards and the company's access number, or through one's mobile phone. Direct dialing is as follows: 001 – country number – area code – local number. The national number of the US and Canada is 1, Ireland 353, Australia 61, New Zealand 64, and UK 44. Omit the 0 from the area code when dialing.

Could I use your phone, please?	*Anata-no denwa-o kashite moratte-mo ee des-ka* あなたの電話を貸してもらってもいいですか。
Do you have a (city/region)...phone directory?	*Denwa-choh arimas-ka* 電話帳ありますか。
Could you find a telephone number for me?	*Denwa-bango-o shirabetay kudasa-i-masen-ka* 電話番号を調べて下さいませんか。
Where can I get a phone card?	*Terehon-kahdo-wa doko-de ka-emas-ka* テレホン・カードはどこで買えますか。
Could you give me...?	*... o oshietay kuda-sigh* …を教えてください。
– the room number...	*...ban-no heya-no denwa-bango* …番の部屋の電話番号
– the international access code	*kok-sigh denwa-no bango* 国際電話の番号
– the country code for...	*... no kuni bango* …の国番号

– the area code for...	*... no shi-gigh kyokuban* …の市外局番
– the number of...	*... no denwa-bango* …の電話番号
Could you check if this number's correct?	*Kono denwa-bango-ga tada-shee-ka. dohka shirabetay kuda-sigh* この電話番号が正しいかどうか調べてください。
Can I dial international direct?	*Gigh-koku-ni chokusetsu dighru dekimas-ka* 外国に直接ダイヤル出来ますか?
Do I have to go through the switchboard?	*Kohkanshu-o tohsh-tay des-ka* 交換手を通してですか。
Do I have to dial '0' first?	*Sigh-sho-ni zero-o mawashimas-ka* 最初にゼロをまわしますか。
Could you dial this number for me, please?	*Kono denwa-bango-ni tsunigh-day kuda-sigh* この電話番号につないで下さい。
Could you put me through to.../extension..., please?	*...ban-ni tsunigh-day kuda-sigh* …番につないでください。
I'd like to place a collect call to...	*...ni korekt-kohru-de denwa-o kake-tigh-n des-nga* …にコレクトコールで電話をかけたいんですが。
What's the charge per minute?	*Ippun-ni-tski ikura des-ka* 一分につきいくらですか。
Have there been any calls for me?	*Watashi-ni denwa-ga arimashta-ka* 私に電話がありましたか。
Could I use my cell phone here?	*Kokode kay-tigh denwa-o tsukattay mo ee-des-ka.* ここで携帯電話を使ってもいいですか。
Do you have a smart phone?	*Sumah-to fon wo motte imas-ka* スマートフォンを持っていますか。
I have lost my SIM card	*Shimu kahdo wo nakushite shimai mashita* SIM カードをなくしてしまいました。

I would like to buy a SIM card	*Shimu kahdo wo kai-tigh no des-ga* SIMカードを買いたいのですが。
The signal is weak here	*Koko-wa denpa-ga yowai des.* ここは電波が弱いです。
Dead zone	*detto zohn* デッドゾーン
My battery is low	*Denchi/batteri ga nakunatte kite imas.* 電池/バッテリーがなくなってきています。
Where can I charge my cell phone?	*Doko-de kay-tigh wo jew-den dekimas-ka* どこで携帯を充電できますか。
Can I text you later?	*Ato-de may-ru shitemo ee-des-ka.* 後でメールしてもいいですか。

The conversation

Hello, this is...	*Mosh moshi, ... des* もしもし、…です。
Who is this, please?	*Donata des-ka* どなたですか。
Is this...?	*... san des-ka* …さんですか。
I'm sorry, I've dialed the wrong number	*Sumimasen-nga, machi-gattay dighru shimashta* すみませんが、間違ってダイヤルしました。
I can't hear you	*Denwa-ga tohkutay, kikoe-nikui des-nga* 電話が遠くて、聞こえにくいんですが。
Excuse me, I don't speak Japanese	*Sumimasen-ga, nihongo-ga wakarimasen* すみませんが、日本語が分かりません。
Is...there please?	*... san irasha-i-mas-ka* …さんいらっしゃいますか。
Is there anybody who speaks English?	*Aygo-ga dekiru shto irasha-i-mas-ka* 英語が出来る人いらっしゃいますか。

Extension..., please	*Nigh-sen bango wo o-ne-gig shimas.* 内線番号をお願いします。
Could you ask him/her to call me back?	*Ato-de denwa-o shtay kureru-yoh o-ne-gigh shimas* 後で電話をしてくれるようお願いします。
My name's... My number's...	*Watashi-no na-migh-wa ... des.* *Watashi-no denwa-bango-wa ... des* 私の名前は…です。私の電話番号は…です。
Could you tell him/her I called?	*Watashi-wa denwa-o kaketa-to tsuta-etay kuda-sigh* 私が電話をかけたと伝えて下さい。
I'll call back tomorrow	*Ashta mata denwa-o kakemas* 明日また電話をかけます。

電話です。	There's a phone call for you
最初に0をダイヤルしてください。	You have to dial '0' first
ちょっと待って下さい。	One moment, please
通じません。	There's no answer
話し中です。	The line's busy
番号が違っています。	You've got a wrong number
今留守です。	He's/she's not here right now
…時に戻ります。	He'll/she'll be back at…

9.3 Internet/email

インターネット Internet	ソーシャルネットワーキング social networking	ツイート/つぶやき tweet
Eメール email	スマートフォン / スマホ smart phone	アダプター adapter
メール texting		充電器 charger

ホットスポット hotspot	インターネットカフェ cybercafé	ログインページ log-in page
ユーザー名 username	電了書籍 / イ　ブック e-book	ウィルス virus
パスワード password	タブレット型パソコン tablet PC	マルウェア malware
ログオン/ログオフ log on/log off	アプリ APP	ハッカー hacker
ウェブサイト web site	アプリケーション application	(ソフトウェアの) 　開発者 developer
ブラウザ browser	クラウド cloud computing	無線LAN/Wi-fi wi-fi
サーチエンジン search engine	ソフトウェア software	搭載（とうさい） built-in
アットマーク @	モバイルバンキング mobile banking	Wi-fi搭載デジカメ wi-fi built-in 　digital camera
ドット dot	ラップトップ laptop	

私のメールは届きましたか。	Did you receive my email?
メールを送信したいのですが。	I'd like to send an email.
メールをチェックしたいのですが、 　このコンピュータで出来ますか。	I'd like to access my email. 　Can I do it on this computer?
ログオンの仕方を教えてくれま 　せんか。	Would you show me how to 　log on?
このへんにインターネットカフェ 　はありますか。	Is there a cybercafé around 　here?
インターネットに繋がりません。 　無線LAN/Wifi がありますか。	I cannot get online. Is there 　Wifi here?
ネットワーク名は何ですか。	What is the network name?
パスワードは何ですか。	What is the password?
ブログを更新しました	I updated my blog.

いいえ、忙しくありませんよ。
ただインターネット をしているだけですから。

No, I am not busy. I am just surfing the web for now.

どのブラウザを使っていますか。

Which browser do you usually use?

フェイスブックで友達になりませんか。

Can we become friends on Facebook?

フェイスブックのIDは何ですか。

What is your Facebook ID?

ツイッターをやっていますか。

Do you use Twitter?

ツイッターのユーザー名は何ですか。

What is your Twitter handle [username]?

よくツイッターでつぶやきますか。

Do you tweet often?

ツイッターでフォローしてもいいですか。

Can I follow you on Twitter?

10 Shopping

10. Shopping

● **Shops usually open around 10am and close around 8pm.**
Department stores close between 6pm and 7pm, depending
on the store and the day. All shops close one day per week.
Neighborhood shops, with the exception of supermarkets, tend
to close on Sundays. Large department stores are always open on
Saturdays and Sundays, but close for one day during the week
except at busy times in July and December. 'Convenience stores'
which remain open 24 hours a day can now be found in most
urban localities. Discount stores offer mainstream goods at up to
40% cheaper than the department stores. There is a sales tax of
5% on all items; this is added to the final bill and is not included
in the price displayed. Bargaining is not the norm in Japan,
and attempts to do so will generally be met by a flat refusal.
It is customary for shop assistants to greet customers with the
greeting *irasshaimase* (welcome).

デパート department store	百均 100-yen store	自転車屋 bicycle repairs
雑貨屋 household goods	喫茶店 coffee house/café	スーパー supermarket
スポーツ用品店 sports shop	八百屋 greengrocer	店 shop
古物屋 second-hand goods	果物屋 fruit shop	レコード屋 record shop
自転車屋 bicycle shop	貴金属店／宝石店 jeweler	毛皮専門店 leather shop
酒屋 liquor shop	おもちゃ屋 toy shop	洋品店 clothes shop
靴屋 shoe shop	花屋 florist	牛乳屋 dairy
肉屋 butcher	コインランドリー launderette	瀬戸物屋 china wear

骨董店／
 アンティーク
antiques

商店街
shopping arcade

食料品店
food shop

ケーキ屋
cake shop

タバコ屋
tobacconist

薬局
pharmacist

金物屋
hardware shop

キオスク／売店
kiosk

みやげ物店
souvenir shop

健康食料品店
health food shop

本屋
bookshop

巾場／マーケット
market

眼鏡屋
optician

パン屋
bakery

美容院
beauty parlor

床屋
hairdresser

香水店
perfume shop

魚屋
fish market

のみの市
flea market

電気屋
electrical
 appliances

お菓子屋
candy shop

日曜大工店
Do-it-yourself store

クリーニング屋
dry cleaner

総菜屋／
 デリカテッセン
delicatessen

コンビニ
convenience store

電気屋
electronics shop

古本屋
used bookstore

アニメ・ゲームショップ
anime/game store

コスプレショップ
cosplay shop

メイドカフェ
maid café

10.1 Shopping conversations

Where can I get...?

... wa dono mise-ni arimas-ka
…はどの店にありますか。

Whcn docs this shop
 open?

Kono mise-wa its akimas-ka
この店はいつ開きますか。

Could you help me,
 please? I'm looking for...

*Sumimasen-nga, ... ga hoshee-n
des-nga*
すみませんが、…がほしいんですが。

Could you tell me where
 the...department is?

... uriba-wa doko des-ka
…売場はどこですか。

Do you sell English newspapers?	*Eigo-no shimbun-mo arimas-ka* 英語の新聞もありますか。
...please	*... o kuda-sigh* …を下さい。
I'm just looking	*Chotto mite-iru dakay des* ちょっと見ているだけです。
I'd also like...	*... mo kuda-sigh* …も下さい。
Could you show me...?	*... o misetay kuda-sigh* …を見せて下さい。
Do you have something...?	*... no-wa arimasen-ka* …のはありませんか。
– less expensive?	*motto ya-sui* もっと安い
– something smaller?	*motto chee-sigh* もっと小さい
– something larger?	*motto oh-kee* もっと大きい
I'll take this one	*Koray kuda-sigh* これ下さい。
Does it come with instructions?	*Setsumaysho-wa hight-tay imas-ka* 説明書は入っていますか。
It's too expensive	*Chotto taka-sugimas* ちょっと高過ぎます。
Could you keep this for me? I'll come back for it later	*Azukattay kudasa-i-masen-ka. Ato-de tori-ni kimas* あずかって下さいませんか。あとで取りに来ます。
Have you got a bag for me, please?	*Bineeru bukuro arimas-ka* ビニール袋ありますか。
Could you gift wrap it, please?	*Prezento des-kara, ts-tsunday kuda-sigh* プレゼントですから、包んで下さい。
I don't need a bag.	*Fukuro wa die-job des.* 袋は大丈夫です。

| Can I have a receipt? | *Re-she-tu wo morae maska.*
レシートをもらえますか。 |

すみませんが、ありません。	I'm sorry, we don't have that
すみませんが、売切れです。	I'm sorry, we're sold out
支払い所でお支払いください。	You can pay at the cash desk
クレジットカードは使えません。	We don't accept credit cards
旅行用小切手は使えません。	We don't accept traveler's checks
外貨は使えません。	We don't accept foreign currency

10.2 Food

I'd like a hundred grams of..., please	*... o hyaku gram o-negigh-shimas* …を100グラムお願いします。
– five hundred grams/ half a kilo of...	*... o gohyaku-gram* …を500グラム
– a kilo of...	*... o ichi-kiro* …を1キロ
Could you...it for me, please?	*... kuda-sigh* …下さい。
Could you slice it/chop it for me, please?	*Usuku/sigh-nomay-ni kittay kuda-sigh* 薄く／さいの目に切って下さい。
Could you grate it for me, please?	*Oroshtay kuda-sigh* おろしてください。
Can I order it?	*Choomon dekimas-ka* 注文出来ますか。
I'll pick it up tomorrow/at...	*Ashta/... ji-ni tori-ni kimas* あした／…時に取りに来ます。
Can you eat this?	*Tabemono des-ka* 食べ物ですか。
Can you drink this?	*Nomimono des-ka* 飲み物ですか。

| What's in it? | *Zigh-ryoh-wa nan des-ka* |
| | 材料は何ですか。 |

10.3 Clothing and shoes

I'd like something to go with this	*Nani-ka kore-ni ni-au-no-ga hoshee-n des-nga*
	何かこれに似合うのがほしいんですが。
Do you have shoes to match this?	*Kore-ni ni-au kuts-ga arimas-ka*
	これに似合う靴がありますか。
I'm a size...in the U.S.	*Amerika no ... sighz nan des-nga*
	アメリカの…サイズなんですが。
Can I try this on?	*Shi-chaku dekimas-ka*
	試着出来ますか。
Where's the fitting room?	*Shi-chaku-shits-wa doko des-ka*
	試着室はどこですか。
It doesn't fit	*Kono sighz-wa igh-masen*
	このサイズは合いません。
This is the right size	*Kono sighz-wa digh-johbu des*
	このサイズは大丈夫です。
It doesn't suit me	*Ni-igh imasen*
	似合いません。
The heel's too high/low	*Kakato-ga taka-sugimas/hiku-sugimas*
	かかとが高過ぎます／低過ぎます。
Is this/are these genuine leather?	*Kore-wa hontoh-no kawa des-ka*
	これは本当の皮ですか。
I'm looking for a...for a three-year-old child	*San-sigh-no kodomo-no tame-ni ... ga hoshee-n des-nga*
	3歳の子供のために…がほしいんですが。
I'd like a silk...	*Kinu-no ... o-negigh shimas*
	絹の…お願いします。

– cotton...	*Momen-no ... o-negigh shimas* 木綿の…お願いします。
– woolen...	*Wooru-no ... o-negigh shimas* ウールの…お願いします。
– linen...	*Asa-no ... o-negigh shimas* 麻の…お願いします。
What temperature can I wash it at?	*Sentaku ondo-wa nando des-ka* 洗濯温度は何度ですか。
Will it shrink in the wash?	*Arat-tara, chijimi-mas-ka* 洗ったら、縮みますか。

濡れたまま干して 下さい。 Drip dry	洗濯機で洗えます。 Machine wash ドライクリーニング にして下さい。	アイロンをかけ ないで下さい。 Do not iron
手で洗って下さい。 Hand wash	Dry clean	

At the cobbler

Could you mend these shoes?	*Kono kutsu-o, shoori dekimas-ka* この靴を修理出来ますか。
Could you put new soles/heels on these?	*Atara-shee kuts-zoko/kakato-o* *ts-kuttay kuda-sigh* 新しい靴底／かかとを作ってください。
When will they be ready?	*Its dekimas-ka* いつできますか。
I'd like..., please	*... o-negigh shimas* …お願いします。
– a tin of shoe polish	*kuts-kreem* 靴クリーム
– a pair of shoelaces	*kutsu-himo* 靴ひも

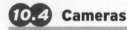

10.4 Cameras

 Shopping

10

| 一眼レフカメラ
single-lens reflex
(SLR) camera
デジカメ
digital camera
デジタル一眼レフ
digital single-lens
reflex camera
画素
pixel | SDカード
SD card
光学ズーム
optical zoom
顔認識カメラ
face-recognition
camera
高画質型デジカメ
high-definition-
digital camera | 画像処理
photo-editing
手ぶれ補正機能
camera shake
correction feature
動画
video |

I'd like to print out photos from my digital camera. Where can I do it?
Deji-kame no shashin wo insatsu she-tigh no des-ga, doko-de deki mas ka.
デジカメの写真を印刷したいのですが、どこで出来ますか。

Can you upload your photos to Facebook?
Shashin-wo feisu bukku ni appu-road shite kure-masen-ka.
写真をフェースブックにアップロードしてくれませんか。

Problems

Could you load the film for me, please?
Kono kamera-ni firum-o iretay kuda-sigh
このカメラにフィルムを入れて下さい。

Could you take the film out for me, please?
Firum-o tori-dashtay kuda-sigh
フィルムを取り出して下さい。

Should I replace the batteries?
Batteree-o tori-kae-nakereba-narimasen-ka
バッテリーを取り換えなければなりませんか。

The...is broken
... ga kowaremashta
…がこわれました。

Could you have a look at my camera, please? It's not working	*Kono kamera-o mitay kuremasen-ka. tsuka-enaku-nattay shimaimashta* このカメラを見てくれませんか。使えなくなってしまいました。
The film's jammed	*Firum-ga ugoki-masen* フィルムが動きません。
The film's broken	*Firum-ga kiremashta* フィルムが切れました。
The flash isn't working	*Furash-ga tentoh shimasen* フラッシュが点灯しません。

Processing and prints

I'd like to have this film developed, please	*Kono firum-o genzoh shtay kuda-sigh* このフィルムを現像してください。
– printed, please	*Kono firum-o print shtay kuda-sigh* このフィルムをプリントしてください。
I'd like...prints from each negative	*Kono nega-o ... migh-zuts print shtay kuda-sigh* このネガを…枚ずつプリントして下さい。
glossy/matte	*kohtaku-no aru/kohtaku-no nigh* 光沢のある／光沢のない
I'd like to have this photo enlarged	*Kore-o hiki-nobashtay kuda-sigh* これを引き伸ばして下さい。
How much is...?	*... wa ikura des-ka* …はいくらですか。
– processing?	*genzoh* 現像
– printing	*print* プリント
– the enlargement	*hiki-nobashi* 引き伸ばし
When will they be ready?	*Its dekimas-ka* いつできますか。

10.5 At the hairdresser

Do I have to make an appointment?	*Yoyak shi-nakereba narimasen-ka* 予約しなければなりませんか。
How long will I have to wait?	*Dono gurigh machimas-ka* どのぐらい待ちますか。
I'd like a...	*Kami-o ... kuda-sigh* 髪を…下さい。
– shampoo	*arattay* 洗って
– haircut	*kittay* 切って
I'd like a shampoo for... please	*... yoh-no shampoo o-negigh shimas* …用のシャンプーお願いします。
– oily hair	*abura-no oh-ee kami* あぶらの多い髪
– dry hair	*kansoh shita kami* 乾燥した髪
– permed hair	*pahma-o waketa kami yoh no shampoo* パーマをかけた髪用のシャンプー
– colored hair	*someta kami* 染めた髪
I'd like an anti-dandruff shampoo	*F-kay bohshi-yoh-no shampoo o-negigh shimas* ふけ防止用のシャンプーお願いします。
– a color rinse shampoo	*karah shampoo o-negigh shimas* カラーシャンプーお願いします。
I want to keep it the same color	*Kono iro-to onaji-ni shtay kuda-sigh* この色と同じにして下さい。
I'd like it darker/lighter	*Motto kuroku/akaruku shtay kuda-sigh* もっと黒く／明るくして下さい。
I'd like...	*... o kaketay kuda-sigh* …をかけてください。
I don't want...	*... wa kake-nigh-day kuda-sigh* …はかけないで下さい。

– hair spray	*he-a spray* ヘアスプレー
– gel	*jeru* ジェル
– lotion	*rohshon* ローション
I'd like short bangs	*Ma-e-gami-o miji-kaku kittay kuda-sigh* 前髪を短く切って下さい。
Not too short at the back	*Ushiro-wa mijika-sugi-nigh yoh-ni* 後は短過ぎないように
Not too long here	*Koko-wa naga-sugi-nigh yoh-ni* ここは長過ぎないように
It needs a little taken off	*Skoshi dakay kittay kuda-sigh* 少しだけ切って下さい。
I want a completely different style	*Hoka-no kamigata-ni shitigh-n des* 他の髪型にしたいんです。
Please thin my hair a little bit	*Kami wo sukoshi sui-te kuda-sigh* 髪を少しすいてください。
I'd like it the same...	*... no yoh-na kamigata-ni shitigh-n des-nga* …のような髪型にしたいんですが…
– as that lady's	*ano kata* あの方
– as in this photo	*kono shashin* この写真
Could you turn the drier up a bit?	*Drighyah-o takaku shtay kuda-sigh* ドライヤーを高くして下さい。
Could you turn the drier down a bit?	*Drighyah-o hikuku shtay kuda-sigh* ドライヤーを低くして下さい。
I'd like...	*... o shtay kuda-sigh* …をして下さい。
– a manicure	*manikyua* マニキュア
– a massage	*massahji* マッサージ

どんな髪型がいいんですか。	What style did you have in mind?
どんな色がいいんですか。	What color did you want it?
温度はよろしいですか。	Is the temperature all right for you?
雑誌をお読みになりますか。	Would you like something to read?
何かお飲みになりますか。	Would you like a drink?
これでよろしいですか。	Is this what you had in mind?

Could you trim...	*... o kiri-soroetay kuda-sigh* …を切りそろえて下さい。
– my bangs?	*ma-e-gami* 前髪
– my beard?	*higay* ひげ
– my moustache?	*kuchi-higay* 口ひげ
I'd like a shave, please	*Hige-o sottay kuda-sigh* ひげを剃って下さい。
I'd like a wet shave, please	*Hige-sori-yoh kamisori-de sottay kuda-sigh* ひげ剃り用カミソリで剃って下さい。

11 Tourist Activities

11. Tourist Activities

The Japan National Tourist Office (JNTO) provides information in English in Tokyo and Kyoto and at Narita Airport. There is also a Travel Phone service offering tourist information and language assistance in English during business hours. In smaller places, information centers are usually located at the railway station.

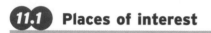 Places of interest

Most museums, tourist sites, and nationally famous temples and gardens charge entrance fees, which average around 400–600 yen for adults. If possible, wear shoes that can be slipped on and off easily, since many tourist attractions, particularly temples and old buildings, require shoes to be removed at the entrance.

Where's the Tourist Information center, please?	*Kankoh an-nigh-sho-wa doko des-ka* 観光案内所はどこですか。
Do you have a city map?	*Machi-no chizu arimas-ka* 町の地図ありますか。
Could you give me some information about...?	*... ni tsuitay oshietay kuda-sigh* …について教えて下さい。
How much is that?	*Ikura des-ka* いくらですか。
What are the main places of interest?	*Omo-ni doko-ga omoshiro-i des-ka* 主にどこが面白いですか。
Could you point them out on the map?	*Chizu-de sashtay kuda-sigh* 地図で指して下さい。
What do you recommend?	*Nani-ka osusume-wa* 何かおすすめは。
We'll be here...	*Koko-ni ... imas* ここに…います。

– for a few hours	*ni, san jikan* 二、三時間
– a day	*ichi-nichi* 一日
– a week	*is-shoo-kan* 一週間
We're interested in...	*... ni kyohmi-ga arimas-ka* …に興味がありますが。
Is there a scenic walk around the city?	*Shinigh kankoh arimas-ka* 市内観光ありますか。
How long does it take?	*Dono gurigh jikan-ga kakarimas-ka* どのぐらい時間がかかりますか。
Where does it start/end?	*Shuppats-ten/shooten-wa doko des-ka* 出発点／終点はどこですか。
Are there any boat cruises here?	*Yooransen ga arimas-ka* 遊覧船がありますか。
Where can we board?	*Doko-de fune-ni noremas-ka* どこで船に乗れますか。
Are there any bus tours?	*Kankoh bas ga arimas-ka* 観光バスがありますか。
Where do we get on?	*Doko-de bas-ni noremas-ka* どこでバスに乗れますか。
Is there a guide who speaks English?	*Aygo-no gighd-ga imas-ka* 英語のガイドがいますか。
What trips can we take around the area?	*Doko-ka tanoshee shoh-ryokoh-wa arimas-ka* どこか楽しい小旅行はありますか。
Are there any excursions?	*Kankoh-tsuah-ga arimas-ka* 観光ツアーがありますか。
Where do they go to?	*Doko-e ikimas-ka* どこへ行きますか。
We'd like to go to...	*... e ikitigh-n des-nga* …へ行きたいんですが
How long is the trip?	*Tsuah-wa nan-jikan kakarimas-ka* ツアーは何時間かかりますか。

How long do we stay in...?	*... ni-wa dono kurigh tigh-zigh shimas-ka* …にはどのくらい滞在しますか。
Are there any guided tours?	*Gighd-tski-tsua-ga arimas-ka* ガイド付きツアーがありますか。
How much free time will we have there?	*Dono-gurigh jiyoo jikan-ga arimas-ka* どのぐらい自由時間がありますか。
We want to go hiking	*Highking-ni iki-tigh-n des-nga* ハイキングに行きたいんですが。
Can we hire a guide?	*Gighd-o tanomemas-ka* ガイドをたのめますか。
Can I book mountain huts?	*Yama-goya-ga yoyaku dekimas-ka* 山小屋が予約出来ますか。
What time does...open?	*Nanji-ni ... ga akimas-ka* 何時に…が開きますか。
What time does...close?	*Nanji-ni ... ga shimarimas-ka* 何時に…が閉まりますか。
What days is...open?	*Nanyohbi-ni ... ga igh-tay imas-ka* 何曜日に…が開いていますか。
What days is...closed?	*Nanyohbi-ni ... ga shimat-tay imas-ka* 何曜日に…が閉まっていますか。
What's the admission price?	*Nyoojoh-ryoh-wa ikura des-ka* 入場料はいくらですか。
Is there...	*... no waribiki kippu arimas-ka* …の割引切符ありますか。
– a group discount?	*groop* グループ
– a child discount?	*kodomo* 子供
– a discount for seniors?	*rokujoo-go-sigh ijoh* 65歳以上
Can I film here?	*Satsu-ay shtay-mo ee des-ka* 撮影してもいいですか。

Can I take (flash) photos?	*(frash-de) Shashin-o totte-mo ee des-ka*
	（フラッシュで）写真を撮ってもいいですか。
Do you have any postcards of...?	*... no eha-gaki-ga arimas-ka*
	…の絵葉書がありますか。
Do you have an English...?	*Aygo-no ... arimas-ka*
	英語の…ありますか。
– catalogue?	*katarog*
	カタログ
– program?	*program*
	プログラム
– brochure?	*panfretto*
	パンフレット

 Going out

Information about entertainment appears in the English language newspapers and in the visitors' guides which can be picked up in hotels. In Tokyo there is a Teletourist service which provides information about events and entertainment in English. Evening dress is rarely worn to the theater. Shows open earlier than in Europe, usually 6.30 or 7.00. Traditional theatre includes *Kabuki, No,* and *Bunraku.* Films generally are shown in the language of origin with Japanese subtitles.

Do you have this week's/ month's entertainment guide?	*Konshoo/kongets-no program arimas-ka*
	今週／今月のプログラムありますか。
What's on tonight?	*Komban-no program-wa doh des-ka*
	今晩のプログラムはどうですか。
We want to go to...	*... ni ikitigh-n des-nga*
	…に行きたいんですが
Which films are showing?	*Donna ayga-ga arimas-ka*
	どんな映画がありますか。

What sort of film is that?	*Dono yoh-na ayga des-ka* どのような映画ですか。
rated adult (over 18)	*sayjin ayga* 成人映画
original version	*orijinaru-ban* オリジナル版
subtitled	*jimaku-tski-de* 字幕付きで
dubbed	*fuki-kae-de* 吹替で
Is it a continuous showing?	*Kuri-keashi joh-en shimas-ka* 繰り返し上演しますか。
What's on at...?	*Nani-ka ee ... wa arimas-ka* 何かいい…はありますか。
– the theater?	*shoh* ショー
– the concert hall?	*konsah-to ho-ru* コンサートホール
– the opera?	*opera* オペラ
Where can I find a good disco around here?	*Kono-hen-ni ee disko-wa arimas-ka* この辺にいいディスコはありますか。
Is it members only?	*Kigh-in-dakay des-ka* 会員だけですか。
Where can I find a good nightclub around here?	*Kono-hen-ni ee night-krab-wa arimas-ka* この辺にいいナイト・クラブはありますか。
Is it evening wear only?	*Saysoh-wa hits-yoh des-ka* 正装は必要ですか。
What time does the show start?	*Shoh-wa nanji-kara des-ka* ショーは何時からですか。

11.3 Booking tickets

Could you reserve...?	*Yoyaku dekimas-ka* 予約出来ますか。
– some tickets	*chiketto* チケット
– a seat in the orchestra	*ik-kigh-seki-de* 一階席で
– a seat in the balcony	*ni-kigh-seki-de* 二階席で
– box seats	*boks-seki-de* ボックス席で
– a table at the front	*zempoh-de* 前方で
– in the middle	*naka-goro-de* 中ごろで
– at the back	*koh-hoh-de* 後方で
Could I reserve...seats for the...o'clock performance?	*... ji-no joh-en-no kippu-o ... migh yoyaku dekimas-ka* …時の上演の切符を…枚予約出来ますか。
Are there any seats left for tonight?	*Komban-no kippu-wa mada arimas-ka* 今晩の切符はまだありますか。
How much is a ticket?	*Ichimigh ikura des-ka* 一枚いくらですか。
When can I pick the tickets up?	*Kippu-wa its morae-mas-ka* 切符はいつもらえますか。
I've got a reservation	*Yoyaku shimashta* 予約しました。
My name's...	*Watashi-no na-migh-wa ... des* 私の名前は…です。

どの上演に予約したいんですか。	Which performance do you want to reserve for?
どんな座席がほしいんですか。	Where would you like to sit?
すみませんが、売切れです。	Everything's sold out
立ち見席だけ残っています。	It's standing room only
二階席だけ残っています。	We've only got balcony seats left
一階席だけ残っています。	We've only got orchestra seats left
前の座席が残っています。	We've only got seats left at the front
後の座席が残っています。	We've only got seats left at the back
何枚ですか。	How many seats would you like?
…時までに切符を取りに来なければなりません。	You'll have to pick up the tickets before...o'clock
切符を見せて下さい。	Tickets, please
こちらの席です。	This is your seat

12 Sports Activities

12. Sports Activities

The most popular spectator sports are baseball, soccer, and *sumo*. There are no public golf courses, but golf driving ranges are found in most places. Public tennis courts get very booked-up. Fitness and sports clubs are widespread.

12.1 Sporting questions

登山 mountain climbing	ヨガ yoga	露天風呂 open-air bath
ハイキング hiking	パワースポット power spots	混浴 mixed-baths
森林浴 forest bathing	温泉 hot spring	日帰り温泉 day-trip hot spring
スノーボード / スノボ snowboarding		

Where can we... around here?	*Kono-hen-de ... ga dekimas-ka* この辺で…が出来ますか。
Can I hire a...here?	*Koko-de ... ga kari-rare-mas-ka* ここで…が借りられますか。
Can I take...lessons?	*... no ressun-ga uke-rare-mas-ka* …のレッスンが受けられますか。
How much is that per hour/per day/a turn?	*Ichi-jikan/ichinichi/ik-kigh ikura des-ka* 一時間／一日／一回いくらですか。
Do I need a permit for that?	*Kyokasho-ga hits-yoh des-ka* 許可書が必要ですか。
Where can I get the permit?	*Kyokasho-wa doko-de hak-koh saremas-ka* 許可書はどこで発行されますか。

私の趣味は登山です。	My hobby is mountain climbing.
ハイキングをするならどこがいいですか。	Where is the good place to go hiking?
登山をするならどこがいいですか。	Where is the good place to go mountain climbing?
有名なパワースポットがこのへんにありますか。	Is there a famous "power spot" around here?
このへんに良い温泉はありますか。	Is there a good hot spring around here?
ここから一番近い日帰り温泉はどこですか。	Which day-trip hot spring is the closest from here?
露天風呂はどこですか。	Where is the open-air bath?
混浴するときの決まりは何ですか。	What are the rules for using the mixed baths?
混浴するときは、何か着ないといけませんか。	Do we have to wear something when going to the mixed baths?

12.2 By the waterfront

Is it a long way to
the sea still?
Kigh-gan maday mada toh-i des-ka
海岸までまだ遠いですか。

Is there ...around here?
Kono hen-ni ... wa arimas-ka
この辺に…はありますか。

– a swimming pool
pooru
プール

– a sandy beach
sunahama
砂浜

– mooring
f-toh
埠頭

Are there any rocks here?
Kono-hen-ni-wa iwa-ga arimas-ka
この辺には岩がありますか。

When's high/low tide?
Its manchoh/kanchoh des-ka
いつ満潮／干潮ですか。

What's the water temperature?	*Swee-on-wa nando des-ka* 水温は何度ですか。
Is it (very) deep here?	*(totemo) Fu-kigh des-ka* （とても）深いですか。
Can you stand here?	*Tatemas-ka* 立てますか。
Is it safe (for children) to swim here?	*(kodomo-ga) Anzen-ni oyogemas-ka* （子供が）安全に泳げますか。
Are there any currents?	*Nagare-wa kitsui des-ka* 流れはきついですか。
Are there any rapids/ waterfalls in this river?	*Kono kawa-ni kyooryoo/taki-ga arimas-ka* この川に急流／滝がありますか。
What does that flag/ buoy mean?	*Ano hata/bui-wa doh yoo imi des-ka* あの旗／ブイはどういう意味ですか。

つり場 Fishing water	要許可書 Permits only	サーフィン禁止 No surfing
危険／注意 Danger	遊泳禁止 No swimming	つり禁止 No fishing

12.3 In the snow

Can I take ski lessons here?	*Koko-de skee-ga naraemas-ka* ここでスキーのレッスンが受けられますか。
for beginners/advanced	*shoshinsha / joh-kyoo* 初心者／上級
How large are the groups?	*Groop-wa nannin-gurigh des-ka* グループは何人ぐらいですか。
What language are the classes in?	*Nanigo-de oshie-raremas-ka* 何語で教えられますか。
I'd like a lift pass, please	*Rift-no ichinichi-ken-o kuda-sigh* リフトの一日券を下さい。

Must I give you a passport photo?	*Shoh-may shashin-ga irimas-ka* 証明写真がいりますか。
Where can I have a passport photo taken?	*Doko-de shoh-may shashin-o tottay moraemas-ka* どこで証明写真を撮ってもらえますか。
Where are the beginners' slopes?	*Shoshinsha no gerenday-wa doko des-ka* 初心者のゲレンデはどこですか。
Are there any runs for cross-country skiing?	*Kono hen-de kros-kantree-skee-ga dekimas- ka* この辺でクロスカントリースキーができますか。
Are the...in operation?	*... wa ugoitay-imas-ka* …は動いていますか。
– ski lifts	*skeerift* スキーリフト
– chair lifts	*rift* リフト
Are the slopes usable?	*Gerenday-wa kakkoh kanoh des-ka* ゲレンデは滑降可能ですか。

13 Health Matters

13. Health Matters

Hospitals or clinics with English-speaking staff can be found in most large cities. Because of the high cost of medical and dental treatment, insurance is advised when travelling. There are pharmacies in every neighborhood and they are easily found.

 Calling a doctor

Could you call/get a doctor quickly, please?	*Hayaku o-isha-san-o yonday/tsretay-kitay kuda-sigh* 早くお医者さんを呼んで／連れてきて下さい。
When does the doctor have office hours?	*O-isha-san-no shinsats-jikan-wa its des-ka* お医者さんの診察時間はいつですか。
When can the doctor come?	*O-isha-san-wa its koremas-ka* お医者さんはいつ来れますか。
I'd like to make an appointment to see the doctor	*O-isha-san-no yoyaku-o shtay kuda-sigh* お医者さんの予約をして下さい。
I've got an appointment to see the doctor at...	*Watashi-wa ... ji-ni o-isha-san-ni au yakusoku-ga arimas* 私は…時にお医者さんに会う約束があります。
Which doctor (druggist) has night/weekend duty?	*Dono isha (yak-kyoku)-ga yakin/shoomats kimmu des-ka* どの医者（薬局）が夜勤／週末勤務ですか。

13.2 What's wrong?

I don't feel well	*Gu-igh-ga waru-i-n des* 具合が悪いんです。

I'm dizzy	*Me-migh-ga shimas* めまいがします。
– ill	*Byohki des* 病気です。
– sick	*Kibun-ga waru-i-n des* 気分が悪いんです。
I've got a cold	*Kazay des* 風邪です。
It hurts here	*Koko-ga i-tigh-n des* ここが痛いんです。
I've been throwing up	*Modoshtay shimatta-n des* もどしてしまったんです。
I'm running a temperature of...degrees	*... do-no nets-ga arimas* …度の熱があります。
I've been stung	*... ni sasare-mashta* …に刺されました。
– by a hornet	*suzume-bachi* スズメバチ
– by an insect	*mushi* 虫
– by a jellyfish	*kuragay* クラゲ
I've been bitten	*... ni kamare-mashta* …に噛まれました。
– by a dog	*inu* 犬
– by a snake	*hebi* 蛇
– by an animal	*dohbuts* 動物
I've cut myself	*Kiri-kizu-o tskemashta* 切り傷をつけました。
I've burned myself	*Yakedo-o shimashta* やけどをしました。

I've grazed myself	*Hada-o suri-muki-mashta* 肌をすりむきました。
I've had a fall	*Korobimashta* ころびました。
I've sprained my ankle	*Ashi-kubi-o kujikimashta* 足首をくじきました。

13.3 The consultation

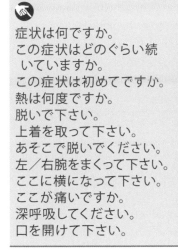

症状は何ですか。	What seems to be the problem?
この症状はどのぐらい続いていますか。	How long have you had these symptoms?
この症状は初めてですか。	Have you had this trouble before?
熱は何度ですか。	How high is your temperature?
脱いで下さい。	Get undressed, please
上着を取って下さい。	Strip to the waist, please
あそこで脱いでください。	You can undress there
左／右腕をまくって下さい。	Roll up your left/right sleeve, please
ここに横になって下さい。	Lie down here, please
ここが痛いですか。	Does this hurt?
深呼吸してください。	Breathe deeply
口を開けて下さい。	Open your mouth

Patients' medical history

I'm a diabetic	*Toh-nyoh-byoh des* 糖尿病です。
I have a heart condition	*Shinzoh-byoh des* 心臓病です。
I have asthma	*Shinzoh-byoh des* 喘息病です。
I'm allergic to...	*... ni tigh-shtay arerugee des* …に対してアレルギーです。

I'm...months pregnant	*... kagetsu-no ninshin des* …何ヶ月の妊娠です。
I'm on a diet	*Shokuji saygen-o shtay imas* 食事制限をしています。
I'm on medication/ the pill	*Kusuri/piru-o tskattay imas* 薬／ピルを使っています。
I've had a heart attack once before	*Shinzoh mahi-o okoshta koto-ga arimas* 心臓麻痺をおこしたことがあります。
I've had a(n)...operation	*... no shujuts-o ukemashta* …の手術を受けました。
I've been ill recently	*Sigh-kin maday byohki deshta* 最近まで病気でした。
I've got an ulcer	*Kigh-yoh-ga arimas* 潰瘍があります。
I've got my period	*Seiri-chu des* 生理中です。

何かに対してアレルギー がありますか。	Do you have any allergies?
薬を使っていますか。	Are you on any medication?
食事制限をしていますか。	Are you on a diet?
妊娠中ですか。	Are you pregnant?
破傷風の予防接種をしま したか。	Have you had a tetanus injection?

The diagnosis

深刻なものではありません。	It's nothing serious
…が骨折しています。	Your ...is broken
…にあざがあります。	You've got a/some bruised...
…をくじいています。	You've got (a) torn...

炎症を起こしています。	You've got an infection
虫垂炎を起こしています。	You've got appendicitis
気管支炎を起こしています。	You've got bronchitis
性病です。	You've got a venereal disease
流行性感冒です。	You've got the flu
心臓麻痺でした。	You've had a heart attack
（ビールス／バクテリアに）感染しています。	You've got an infection (viral.../bacterial...)
肺炎です。	You've got pneumonia
潰瘍があります。	You've got an ulcer
筋をひきちがえました。	You've pulled a muscle
腟の感染症です。	You've got a vaginal infection
食中毒です。	You've got food poisoning
日射病です。	You've got sunstroke
…に対してアレルギーがあります。	You're allergic to ...
妊娠です。	You're pregnant
あなたの血液／小便／糞便を検査したいんです。	I'd like to have your blood/urine/stools tested
傷口を縫い合わせなければなりません。	It needs stitches
専門医／病院に紹介します。	I'm referring you to a specialist/sending you to the hospital
X線写真を撮らなければなりません。	You'll need to have some X-rays taken
ちょっと待合室で待っていて下さい。	Could you wait in the waiting room, please?
手術が必要です。	You'll need an operation

Is it contagious?	*Densensay des-ka* 伝染性ですか。
How long do I have to stay...?	*Dono gu-righ nagaku ... ni inakareba narimasen-ka* どのぐらい長く…にいなければなりませんか。
– in bed	*beddo* ベッド

– in the hospital	*byoh-in* 病院
Do I have to go on a special diet?	*Shokuji saygen-o shinakereba narimasen-ka* 食事制限をしなければなりませんか。
Am I allowed to travel?	*Ryokoh shtay-mo ee des-ka* 旅行してもいいですか。
When do I have to come back?	*Its ukagawa-nakereba narimasen-ka* いつ伺わなければなりませんか。
I'll come back tomorrow	*Mata ashta uka-gigh-imas* また明日伺います。

明日／…日後にここにきて下さい。	Come back tomorrow/in ...days' time

13.4 Medications and prescriptions

How do I take this medicine?	*Kono kusuri-wa doh nomimas-ka* この薬はどう飲みますか。
How many pills/drops/ injections/spoonfuls/ tablets each time?	*Ik-kigh dono-kurigh-zuts des-ka* 一回どのくらいずつですか。
How many times a day?	*Ichinichi nankigh-zuts des-ka* 一日何回ずつですか。
I've forgotten my medication. At home I take...	*Kusuri-o wasurete-shimatta-n-des-nga, foodan-wa ... o tskattay imas* 薬を忘れてしまったんですが、普段は…を使っています。
Could you write a prescription for me?	*Shohoh-sen o dashite kudasa-i-masen-ka* 処方箋を出して下さいませんか。

抗生物質／飲み薬／
　トランキライザー／
　鎮痛剤の処方を書きます。
休まなければなりません。
外へ出かけてはいけません。
寝ていなければなりません。

I'm prescribing antibiotics/
　a mixture/a tranquillizer/
　pain killers
Have lots of rest
Stay indoors
Stay in bed

食事前に before meals	…日間 for...days	全部飲んで下さい swallow whole
カプセル capsules	注射 injections	錠剤 tablets
水に溶かす dissolve in water	外用のみ not for internal usc	飲む take
ドロップ drops	軟膏 ointment	この薬は自動車の 　運転に影響を 　きたします。 this medication 　impairs your 　driving
…時間おきに every...hours	つける rub on	
完全に治療を終 　わらせる finish the 　prescription	スプーン（大／小） spoonfuls 　(tablespoons/ 　teaspoons)	一日…回 ...times a day

13.5 At the dentist

Do you know a good
　dentist?

Ee ha-isha-o shtay imas-ka
いい歯医者を知っていますか。

Could you make a
　dentist's appointment
　for me? It's urgent

*Watashi-no tame-ni ha-isha-ni yoyaku
shtay kudasa-i-masen-ka. isoi-day imas*
私のために歯医者に予約して下さい
ませんか。急いでいます。

Can I come in today,
　please?

Kyoh uka-gigh-emas-ka
今日伺えますか。

I have (terrible) toothache	*(sugoku) Ha-ga i-tigh-n des* （すごく）歯が痛いんです。
Could you prescribe/ 　give me a painkiller?	*Chintsoo-zigh-no shohoh-o kaitay* *kuda-sigh/chintsoo-zigh-o kuda-sigh* 鎮痛剤の処方を書いて下さい／鎮痛 剤をください。
A piece of my tooth 　has broken off	*Ha-ga oremashta* 歯がおれました。
My filling's come out	*Ha-ni tsumeta-no-ga toremashta* 歯につめたのがとれました。
I've got a broken crown	*Shikan-ga koware-mashta* 歯冠がこわれました。
I'd like (don't want) a 　local anaesthetic	*Kyokusho maswee-o kaketay* *(kake-nigh-de) kuda-sigh* 局所麻酔をかけて(かけない)ください。
Can you do a temporary 　repair job?	*Ohkyoo chiryo-o shtay kuda-sigh* 応急治療をしてください。
I don't want this tooth 　pulled	*Kono ha-wa nuka-nigh-de kuda-sigh* この歯は抜かないでください。
My dentures are broken. 　Can you fix them?	*Ireba-ga kowaremashta-ga, shoori* *dekimas-ka* 入れ歯がこわれましたが、修理できま すか。

どの歯が痛いんですか。	Which tooth hurts?
はれています。	You've got an abscess
歯茎の治療が必要です。	I'll have to do a root canal
この歯をつめなければ／ 　抜かなければ／けずらな 　ければなりません。	I'll have to fill/pull this tooth/ 　file this...down
穴を開けなければなりません。	I'll have to drill
口を大きく開けて下さい。	Open wide, please
口を閉めて下さい。	Close your mouth, please
口をゆすいで下さい。	Rinse, please
まだ痛いですか。	Does it hurt still?

14 Emergencies

14. Emergencies

Emergency phone numbers: Police: 110; Ambulance/Fire: 119. On a public phone, press the red button and dial; no money is necessary. Speak slowly and clearly if there is no Japanese speaker with you. If you are in difficulty you can ring the Travel Phone service and speak to someone in English; insert 10 yen and dial 106 and in English say to the operator 'Collect call TIC'. The coin will be returned.

14.1 Asking for help

Help!	*Tas-ketay!* 助けて！
Fire!	*Kaji!* 火事！
Police!	*Kay-sats!* 警察！
Quick!	*Hayaku!* 早く！
Danger!	*Abu-nigh!* 危ない！
Watch out!/Be careful!	*Abu-nigh!* あぶない！
Stop!	*Tomaray!* 止まれ！
Don't!	*Shi-nigh-de!/suru-na!* しないで！／するな！
Let go!	*Te-o doketay yo!/Te-o hanashtay!* 手をどけてよ！／手をはなして！
Stop that thief!	*Doroboh-o tometay!* 泥棒を止めて！
Could you help me, please?	*Tas-ketay kuda-sigh* 助けて下さい。

Where's the police station/emergency exit/ fire escape?	*Kaysats-sho/hijoh-guchi/hinan-kigh-dan-wa doko des-ka* 警察署／非常口／避難階段はどこですか。
Where's the fire extinguisher?	*Shohkaki-wa doko-des-ka* 消火器はどこですか。
Call the fire department!	*Shohbohsha-o yonday!* 消防車を呼んで！
Call the police!	*Kaysats-o yonday!* 警察を呼んで！
Call an ambulance!	*Kyookyoosha-o yonday!* 救急車を呼んで！
Where's the nearest phone?	*Denwa-wa doko des-ka* 電話はどこですか。
Could I use your phone?	*Denwa-o ts-kawashtay kuda-sigh* 電話を使わせてください。
What's the number for the police?	*Kay-sats-wa namban des-ka* 警察は何番ですか。

14.2 Lost items

The railways, subway lines, and taxi companies have lost-and-found services.

I've lost my digital camera	*Deji-kame-o naku-shimashta.* デジカメをなくしました。
I've left my cell phone on the train	*Densha-ni kay-tigh wo wasurete shimai mashta.* 電車に携帯を忘れてしまいました。
I've lost my purse/wallet	*Sighfu-o naku-shimashta* 財布をなくしました。
I left my...yesterday	*Kinoh ... o okiwasure-mashta* 昨日…を置き忘れました。
I left my...here	*Koko-ni ... o oki-wasure-mashta* ここに…を置き忘れました。

Did you find my...?	*Watashi-no ... ga mitsukari-mashta-ka*
	私の…が見つかりましたか。
It was right here	*Koko-ni arimashta*
	ここにありました。
It's quite valuable	*Totemo kichoh-hin des*
	とても貴重品です。
Where's the lost and found property office?	*Wasuremono-kakari-wa doko des-ka*
	忘れ物係りはどこですか。

 **14.3** **Accidents**

Robbery and violent crime are rare in Japan. The police maintain a visible presence through a network of small police stations called *koban*, usually found near railway stations. The policemen will help you find an address.

There's been an accident	*Jiko-ga okimashta*
	事故が起きました。
Someone's fallen into the water	*Shto-ga mizu-ni ochimashta*
	人が水に落ちました。
There's a fire	*Kaji des*
	火事です。
Is anyone hurt?	*Kega-o shita shto imas-ka*
	怪我をした人いますか。
Some people have been injured	*Keganin-ga imas*
	怪我人がいます。
No one's been injured	*Keganin-wa imasen*
	怪我人はいません。
There's someone in the car/train still	*Shto-ga mada kuruma/ressha-ni nokottay imas*
	人がまだ車／列車に残っています。
It's not too bad. Don't worry	*Sore-hodo demo arimasen. Shimpigh shi-nigh-de kuda-sigh*
	それほどでもありません。心配しないで下さい。

Leave everything the way it is, please	*Nani-mo sawara-nigh-de kuda-sigh* 何もさわらないで下さい。
I want to talk to the police first	*Mazu kaysats-to hanashi-tigh-n des* まず警察と話したいんです。
I want to take a photo first	*Mazu shashin-o tori-tigh-n des* まず写真を取りたいんです。
Here's my name and address	*Kore-ga watashi-no na-migh-to joosho des* これが私の名前と住所です。
Could I have your name and address?	*Anata-no na-migh-to joosho-o oshietay kuda-sigh* あなたの名前と住所を教えて下さい。
Could I see some identification/your insurance papers?	*Mibun shohmaysho/hokan-shohsho-o misetay kuda-sigh* 身分証明書／保険証書を見せて下さい。
Will you act as a witness?	*Shohnin-ni nattay kuremas-ka* 証人になってくれますか。
I need the details for the insurance	*Hoken-no tame-ni shoh-sigh-ga hits-yoh des* 保険のために詳細が必要です。
Are you insured?	*Hoken-ni hight-tay imas-ka* 保険に入っていますか。
Could you sign here, please?	*Koko-ni sign-o shtay kuda-sigh* ここにサインをして下さい。

 **Theft**

I've been robbed	*Nusu-mare-mashta* 盗まれました。
My...has been stolen	*... ga nusu-mare-mashta* …が盗まれました。

14.5 Missing person

I've lost my child/ grandmother	*Kodomo/sobo-ga mighgo-ni narimashta* 子供／祖母が迷子になりました。
Could you help me find him/her?	*Sagasu-no-o tetsudattay kuda-sigh* 捜すのを手伝って下さい。
Have you seen a small child?	*Chee-sigh ko-o mimashta-ka* 小さい子を見ましたか。
He's/she's...years old	*... sigh des* …歳です。
He's/she's got short/long/ blond/red/brown/black/ gray/curly/straight/ frizzy hair	*Kami-ga miji-kigh/na-gigh/kimpats/ a-kigh/cha-iro/kuro-i/hakuhats/ maki-ge/mas-sugu/chijirege des* 髪が短い／長い／金髪／赤い／茶色／ 黒い／白髪／巻き毛／真っ直ぐ／ 縮れ毛です。
with a ponytail	*ponee-tehru des* ポニーテールで
with braids	*mitsu-ami-de* 三つ編みで
in a bun	*tabanetay* たばねて
He's/she's got blue/ brown eycs	*Me-ga ao-i ... cha-iro des* 目が青い…茶色です。
He's wearing swimming trunks	*Kigh-swee pants-o high-tay imas* 海水パンツをはいています。
...hiking boots	*Tohzan-gutsu-o high-tay imas* 登山靴をはいています。
with glasses	*Meganay-o kaketay imas* 眼鏡をかけています。
tall/short	*oh-kee/chee-sigh* 大きい／小さい
This is a photo of him/her	*Kare ... kanoji-no shashin des* 彼…彼女の写真です。

14.6 The police

An arrest

運転免許証を見せて下さい。	Your driving license, please
スピード違反です。	You were speeding
ここは駐車禁止です。	You're not allowed to park here
ライトがついていません。	Your lights aren't working
罰金は…円です。	That's a...yen fine
今払いますか。	Do you want to pay now?
今払わなければなりません。	You'll have to pay now

I don't speak Japanese

Nihongo-ga hanase-masen
日本語が話せません。

I didn't see the sign

Ano kohtsoo-hyohshiki-ga miemasen deshta
あの交通標識が見えませんでした。

I don't understand
  what it says

Ano hyohshiki-wa wakarimasen
あの標識は分かりません。

I was only doing...
  kilometers an hour

Jisoku ...kiro-dake-de hashittay imashta
時速…キロだけで走っていました。

I'll have my car
  checked

Kuruma-o kensa shte-morigh-mas
車を検査してもらいます。

I was blinded by
  oncoming lights

Tigh-koh-sha-no righto-ni me-ga kurami mashta
対向車のライトに目がくらみました。

At the police station

I want to report a
  collision/missing
  person/rape

Shohtots/mighgo/gohkan-o todoke-ni kimashta
衝突／まい子／強姦を届けに来ました。

Could you make out a
  report, please?

Chohsho-o kigh-tay kuda-sigh
調書を書いて下さい。

どこで起こりましたか。 Where did it happen?
何をなくしましたか。 What's missing?
何が盗まれましたか。 What's been taken?
身分証明書を見せて下さい。 Could I see some identification?
それは何時でしたか。 What time did it happen?
誰が関係しましたか。 Who was involved?
証人がいますか。 Are there any witnesses?
ここに記入してください。 Fill this out, please
ここにサインをして下さい。 Sign here, please
通訳が必要ですか。 Do you want an interpreter?

Could I have a copy for the insurance?	*Hoken-no tame-ni utsushi-o kuda-sigh* 保険のために写しをください。
I've lost everything	*Zembu ushi-nigh-mashta* 全部失いました。
I've lost all my money	*Okane-ga zenbu nakunari-mashta* お金が全部なくなりました。
Could you lend me some money?	*Okane-o skoshi kashtay kuda-sigh-mas-ka* お金を少し貸して下さいますか。
I'd like an interpreter	*Tsooyaku-ga hits-yoh des* 通訳が必要です。
I'm innocent	*Watashi-wa muzigh des* 私は無罪です。
I don't know anything about it	*Nan-ni-mo shirimasen* 何も知りません。
I want to speak to someone	*... no shto-to hanashi-tigh-n des* …の人と話したいんです。
...from the American consulate/ embassy	*amerika ryohjikan/tigh-shikan* アメリカ領事館/大使館
I want a lawyer who speaks English	*Eigo ga hanaseru bengoshi-ga hoshee-n des* 英語が話せる弁護士がほしいんです。

15 English-Japanese Word List

15. English-Japanese Word List

The following word list is meant to supplement the chapters in this book. Where the meaning of the word is very broad, notes have been inserted to show the sense in which the Japanese word is used. Some of the words not contained in this list can be found elsewhere in the book, e.g. alongside the diagrams of the car, bicycle and camping equipment.

A

100 grams	100グラム	hyaku-gram
a little	少し	skosh
about	約／だいたい	yaku/digh-tigh
above	上	ue
abroad	外国	gigh-kok
abundant	豊富な	hohfu-na
accident	事故	jiko
adapter	アダプター	adapu-tah
adder	マムシ	mamushi
addition	計算	kaysan
address	住所	joo-sho
admission	入場	nyoojoh
admission price	入場料	nyoojoh-ryoh
advice	忠告	choo-kok
after	…の後で	… no ato-de
afternoon	午後	gogo
aftershave	アフターシェーブローション	aftah-shayb rohshon
again	もう一度	moh ichido
against	…に対して	… ni tigh-shtay
age	年齢	nen-ray
AIDS	エイズ	ayz
air conditioning	エアコン	e-a-kon
air mattress	エア・マットレス	e-a mattoresu
airplane	飛行機	hikohki
airport	空港	kookoh
airport hotel	空港内ホテル	ku-ko-nigh hoteru
airport security	空港警備／ 空港セキュリティー	ku-ko-keibi/ ku-ko-sekyuritea
aisle seat	通路側の席	tsu-ro gawa no seki
alarm	警告	kay-kok
alarm clock	目覚まし時計	mezamashi-dokay
alcohol	アルコール	aru-kohru
all the time	ずっと	zutto
allergic	アレルギー	areru-gee
alone	一人で	shtori day
always	いつも	its-mo
ambulance	救急車	kyoo-kyoo-sha
America	アメリカ	amerika
American	アメリカ人	amerika-jin
amount	総額	soh-gak

amusement park	遊園地	*yoo-en-chi*
anaesthetize (local)	局所麻酔をかける	*kyokusho-maswee-o kakeru*
anchovy	アンチョビー	*anchobee*
angry	おこった	*okotta*
animal	動物	*doh-buts*
anime/game store	アニメ・ゲームショップ	*anime/game shoppu*
ankle	くるぶし	*kurubushi*
answer	答え／返事	*ko-tigh/henji*
ant	アリ	*ari*
antibiotics	抗生物質	*kohsay busshits*
antifreeze	不凍液	*f-toh-eki*
antique	古代の	*kodigh-no*
antiques	古美術／骨董品	*kobijuts/kottoh-hin*
anus	肛門	*kohmon*
apartment	アパート	*a-pahto*
aperitif	食前酒	*shokuzen-shu*
apologies	許し	*yurushi*
APP	アプリ	*apuri*
apple	リンゴ	*ringo*
apple juice	リンゴジュース	*ringo joos*
apple pie	アップルパイ	*appuru pigh*
apple sauce	アップルソース	*appuru sohsu*
application	アプリケーション	*apuri-kay-shon*
appointment	約束	*yak-soku*
apricot	アンズ	*anzu*
April	四月	*shigats*
architecture	建築	*ken-chiku*
area	環境	*kankyoh*
area code	市外局番	*shi-gigh kyokuban*
arm	腕	*uday*
arrange	約束する	*yak-soku suru*
arrive	着く	*tsuku*
arrow	矢印	*ya-jirushi*
art	芸術	*gay-juts*
artery	動脈	*doh-myaku*
article	物	*mono*
artificial respiration	人口呼吸	*jinkoh kokyoo*
ashtray	灰皿	*high-zara*
ask	尋ねる／問う	*tazuneru/tou*
ask (for)	頼む	*tanomu*
asparagus	アスパラガス	*asparagas*
aspirin	アスピリン	*aspirin*
assault	強姦	*gohkan*
at @	アットマーク	*atto-mah-ku*
at home	家に	*uchi-ni*
at night	夜	*yoru*
at the back	後に	*ushiro-ni*
at the front	前に	*ma-e-ni*
at the latest	遅くても	*osokutemo*
ATM card	キャッシュカード	*cash kah-do*
August	八月	*hachi-gats*
automatic	自動的	*jodoh-teki*
autumn	秋	*aki*
avalanche	雪崩	*nadaray*
awake	起きた	*okita*
awning	日よけ	*hiyokay*

B

baby	赤ちゃん	aka-chan
baby sitter	ベビーシッター	baybee-shittah
back	背中	senaka
backpack	リュックサック	ryukkusakku
bacon	ベーコン	behkon
bad	悪い	waru-i
bad (terrible)	ひどい／大変	hidoi/tigh-hen
bag	カバン	kaban
baggage claim	手荷物受取所	te-nimotsu uke-tori jo
baggage claim check	手荷物引換券	te-nimotsu hiki-kae ken
baker	パン屋	pan-ya
balcony	バルコニー	barukonee
ball	ボール／球	bohru/tama
ballet	バレー	baray
ballpoint pen	ボールペン	bohru-pen
banana	バナナ	banana
bandage	包帯	hoh-tigh
Bandaids	バンソウコウ	bansohkoh
bank	銀行	gin-koh
bangs	前髪	ma-e-gami
bank (river)	岸	kishi
bar (cafe)	バー	bah
bar	バー	bah
barbecue	バーベキュー	bahbekyoo
basketball (to play)	バスケットボール	basketto-bohru
bath	風呂／バス	furo/bas
bath towel	バスタオル	bas-taoru
bathing cap	海水帽	kigh-swee boh
bathing suit	水着	mizu-gi
bathroom	風呂場／バスルーム	furoba/bas-room
battery	バッテリー／電池	betteree/denchi
beach	浜／ビーチ	hama/beechi
beans	豆	mamay
beautiful	すばらしい／華美な	subara-shee/kabi-na
beautiful	美しい／きれいな	utsuku-shee/kiray-na
beauty parlor	美容院	biyoh-in
bed	ベッド／寝台	beddo/shin-digh
bee	ミツバチ	mitsu-bachi
beef	牛肉	gyooniku
beer	ビール	beeru
begin	始まる	haji-maru
beginner	初心者	sho-shin-sha
behind	後	ushiro
belt	ベルト	beruto
berth	寝台	shin-digh
better (to get)	元気になる／快復する	genki-ni naru/kigh-fuku suru
bicarb	重炭酸ソーダ	jootan-san sohda
bicycle	自転車	jitensha
bicycle pump	空気入れ	kooki-iray
bicycle repairman	自転車屋	jitensha-ya
bikini	ビキニ	bikini
bill	勘定	kanjoh
billiards (to play)	玉突きをする	tama-tski-o suru
birthday	誕生日	tanjoh-bi
biscuit	ビスケット／クッキー	bisketto/kukkee
bite	かむ	kamu

bitter	苦い	ni-gigh
black	黒い	kuro-i
bland (taste)	味のない	aji-no nigh
blanket	毛布	mohf
bleach	漂白する／脱色する	hyoh-hak suru/dasshok suru
blister	水膨れ	mizu-buku-ray
blond	金髪	kimpats
blood	血液	kets-eki
blood pressure	血圧	kets-ats
bloody nose	鼻血	hana-ji
blouse	ブラウス	burausu
blow dry	ブロー・ドライ	buroh-drigh
blue	青い	a-oi
blunt	鈍い	nibui
boarding pass	搭乗券	toh-joe-ken
boat	ボート	bohto
body	体	karada
boiled	茹でた	yudeta
boiled ham	ハム	hamu
bonbon	ボンボン	bonbon
bone	骨	honay
bonnet	ボンネット	bon-netto
book	本	hon
booked (theater ticket)	予約した	yoyaku shta
booking office (theater ticket)	プレーガイド	pureh-gighdo
bookshop	本屋	hon-ya
border	国境	kokkyoh
bored (to be)	飽きた	akita
boring	面白くない／つまらない	omoshi-roku-nigh/ tsumara-nigh
born	生まれた	umareta
borrow (from)	…から借りる	... kara kariru
botanical gardens	植物園	shokubutsu-en
both	両方	ryoh-hoh
bottle	びん	bin
bottle (baby's)	哺乳びん	honyoo-bin
bottle-warmer	哺乳びん保温器	honyoo-bin ho-onki
bowling	ボーリングをする	bohring-o suru
box	箱	hako
box office	プレーガイド	pureh-gighdo
box (in theater)	ボックス席で	bokks seki-de
boy	男の子	otoko-no ko
bra	ブラジャー	burajah
bracelet	腕輪／ブレスレット	uday-wa/bures-retto
braised	煮込んだ	nikonda
brake	ブレーキ	brayki
brake oil	ブレーキオイル	brayki-oiru
bread	パン	pan
break	折る	oru
breakfast	朝ご飯	asa-gohan
breast	胸	munay
breast milk	母乳	bonyu
bridge	橋	hashi
briefs	パンツ／パンティー	pants/pantee
bring	持ってくる	mottay kuru
brochure	パンフレット	panfretto

broken	破れた／こわれた	*yabureta/kowareta*
brother (older, other's)	お兄さん	*o-nee-san*
brother (older, own)	兄	*ani*
brother (younger, other's)	弟さん	*o-tohto-san*
brother (younger, own)	弟	*o-tohto*
brown	茶色	*cha-iro*
browser	ブラウザ	*burauza*
bruise	あざができる	*aza-ga dekiru*
brush	ブラシ	*burashi*
Brussels sprouts	芽キャベツ	*me-kyabets*
bucket	バケツ	*baketsu*
bugs	害虫／ばい菌	*gigh-choo/bigh-kin*
building	建物	*tate-mono*
built-in	搭載	*toh-sigh*
bun	菓子パン	*kashi-pan*
buoy	ブイ	*bui*
burglary	押し込み	*oshikomi*
burn	火傷	*yakedo*
burn (verb)	やける	*yakeru*
burnt	焼いた	*yigh-ta*
bus	バス	*bas*
bus station	バスの発着所	*bas-no hachaku-jo*
bus stop	バス停	*bas-tay*
business class	ビジネスクラス	*bijinesu-kuras*
business trip	出張	*shutchoh*
busy (schedule)	忙しい	*isogashee*
busy (traffic)	混雑	*konzats*
butane camping gas	ブタン・ガス	*butan-gas*
butcher	肉屋	*niku-ya*
butter	バター	*batah*
button	ボタン	*botan*
buy	買う	*ka-u*
by airmail	航空便で	*kohkoobin-de*
by phone	電話で	*denwa-de*

C

cabbage	キャベツ	*kyabets*
cabin	船室	*sen-shits*
cake	ケーキ	*kehki*
cake shop	ケーキ屋／お菓子屋	*kayki-ya/okashi-ya*
call	呼び出し	*yobi-dashi*
call (phone)	電話をする	*denwa-o suru*
called (name)	…と言う／…と言います	*... to yoo/... to eemas*
camera	カメラ	*kamera*
camera shake correction (feature)	手ぶれ補正機能	*tebure hosei kinoh*
camp (verb)	キャンプする	*kyampu suru*
camp shop	キャンプ場売店	*kyampu-jo bigh-ten*
camp site	キャンプ場	*kyampu-jo*
camper	キャンピングカー	*kyamping-kah*
campfire	キャンプファイヤー	*kyampu-figh-yah*
camping guide	キャンプ案内	*kyampu an-nigh*
camping permit	キャンプ場使用 許可書	*kyampu-jo shiyoh kyoka-sho*
cancel	取り消す	*tori-kes*
candle	ローソク	*rohsok*
candy	お菓子／おやつ	*okashi/oyats*

canoe	カヌー	ka-noo
car	車／自動車	kuruma/jidoh-sha
car deck	自動車用の甲板	jidoh-sha-yohno kampan
car documents	車の証明書	kuruma-no shohmay-sho
car seat (child's)	ベビーシート	bebee sheeto
car trouble	車の故障	kuruma-no koshoh
caravan	キャラバン	kyaraban
cardigan	カーディガン	kahdigan
careful	注意深い	choo-i-bu-kigh
carrot	にんじん	ninjin
carriage	乳母車／ベビーカー	ubaguruma/baybee-kah
cartridge	カセットフィルム	kasetto-firum
cascade	滝	taki
cash desk	支払い所	shi-harigh-jo
casino	カジノ	kajino
cassette	カセット・テープ	kasetto-tayp
castle	城	shiro
cat	猫	neko
catalogue	カタログ	katarog
cathedral	大聖堂	digh-say-doh
cauliflower	カリフラワー	kari-fura-wah
cave	ほら穴	hora-ana
CD	シーディー	shee-dee
celebrate	祝う	iwau
cell phone	携帯電話/携帯	kay-tigh denwa/kay-tigh
cemetery	墓地	bochi
centimeter	センチ（メートル）	senchi (mehtoru)
central heating	セントラル・ヒーティング	sentoraru-heetingu
center	…の中の	... no naka-no
center (city)	中心地	choo-shin-chi
chair	椅子	isu
chambermaid	ルーム係り	room-gakari
champagne	シャンペン	shanpen
change	変える	kaeru
change (money)	両替	ryoh-gigh
change (money) (verb)	両替する	ryoh-gigh suru
change (trains)	乗り換える	nori-ka-eru
change the baby's diaper	おむつを取り替える	omutsu-o tori-ka-eru
change the oil	オイルを交換する	oiru-o kohkan suru
charger	充電器	ju-den-ki
charter flight	チャーター便	chahtah-bin
chat	言い寄る	ce-yoru
check	チェッカー	chekkah
checked luggage	手荷物一時預かり所	te-nimots ichi-ji azukari-jo
check-in	チェックイン	chekku-in
cheers	乾杯	kam-pigh
cheese	チーズ	cheez
chef	コックさん	kukku-san
check	小切手	kogit-tay
cherries	チェリー／サクランボ	cheree/sakurambo
chess (to play)	チェスをする	chesu-o suru
chewing gum	チューインガム	chooing-gam
chicken	ニワトリ	niwatori
child (other's)	お子さん	okosan
child (own)	子供	kodomo
child's seat	子供用いす	kodomo-yoh isu
chilled	冷たくした	tsumetaku shta

chin	あご	ago
chocolate	チョコレート	choko-rehto
choose	選択する／選ぶ	sentaku suru/erabu
chop (with breadcrumb)	カツレツ	katsuretsu
chop (meat)	挽き肉	hiki-niku
church	教会	kyoh-kigh
church service	礼拝	ray-high
cigar	葉巻	hamaki
cigar shop	たばこ屋	tabakoya
cigarette	たばこ	tabako
circle	円	en
circus	サーカス	sahkas
city	市	shi
clean	清潔な	sayketsu-na
clean (verb)	掃除する	sohji suru
clear	はっきりした	hakkiri shta
clearance (sale)	セール	sayru
clock	時計	to-kay
closed	閉まっている	shmatte-iru
closed off (road)	通行止め	tsoo-koh domay
clothes	衣服	if-ku
clothes hanger	ハンガー／衣紋掛け	han-gah/emon-kakay
clothes pin	洗濯ばさみ	sentaku-basami
clothing	衣類	i-rui
cloud computing	クラウド	kuraudo
coat	コート	kohto
cockroach	ゴキブリ／アブラムシ	gokiburi/abura-mushi
cocoa	ココア	koko-a
cod	タラ	tara
coffee	コーヒー	koh-hee
coffee filter	コーヒー・フィルター	koh-hee firutah
cognac	コニャック	konnyakku
cold	風邪	kazay
cold (not hot)	寒い	samu-i
collarbone	鎖骨	sakots
colleague	同僚	doh-ryoh
collision	衝突	shoh-tots
cologne	化粧水	keshoh-swee
color	色	iro
color pencils	色鉛筆	iro-empits
color television	カラーテレビ	karah-terebi
coloring book	ぬり絵の本	nuri-e-no hon
comb	くし	kushi
come	来る	kuru
come back	戻って来る	modottay kuru
compartment	コンパートメント	konpahtomento
complaint	苦情	kujoh
complaint (illness)	痛み	itami
completely	全く	mattaku
compliment	賛辞	sanji
compulsory	義務	gimu
computer	パソコン	paso-kon
concert (classical)	コンサート	konsahto
concert hall	コンサートホール	konsahto-hohru
concussion	脳しんとう	noh-shintoh
condensed milk	クリーム	kureem
condom	コンドーム	kondohm

congratulate	祝う	iwa-u
connection	接続	setsu-zoku
constipation	便秘	bempi
consulate	領事館	ryohji-kan
consultation (house call by doctor)	往診	ohshin
contact lens	コンタクトレンズ	kontakuto-renzu
contagious	伝染性の	densensay-no
contraceptive	避妊の	hinin-no
contraceptive pill	避妊薬／ピル	hinin-yak/piru
convenience store	コンビニ	kon-bini
cook	コック	kokku
cook (verb)	料理する	ryohri suru
copper	銅	doh
copy	コピー	kopee
corkscrew	コルク栓抜き	koruk-sen-nuki
corn flour	コーンスターチ	kohn-stahchi
corner	隅／角	sumi/kado
correct	正しい	tada-shee
correspond	文通する	bun-tsoo suru
corridor	廊下	rohka
cosplay shop	コスプレショップ	cosplay shoppu
costume	衣装	i-shoh
cot	ベビーベッド	bebee-beddo
cotton	木綿	momen
cotton antiseptic	脱脂綿／綿	dasshi-men/wata
cough	咳	seki
cough (verb)	咳込む	seki-komu
cough syrup	咳止めシロップ	seki-domay shiroppu
counter	受付け	uke-tskay
country (nation)	国	kuni
country (rural area)	田舎	inaka
country code	国番号	kuni ban-go
course (of treatment)	治療	chi-ryoh
cousin	いとこ	itoko
crab	蟹	kani
cream	クリーム	kureem
cream (fresh)	生クリーム	nama-kureemu
credit card	クレジット・カード	kurejitto-kahdo
croissant	クロワッサン	kuro-wasson
cross the road	横断する	ohdan suru
cross-country run	クロスカントリースキー用のコース	kuros-kantoree-skee-yoh no kohs
cross-country skiing	クロスカントリー スキー	kuros-kantoree-skee
cross-country skis	クロスカントリー用 スキー	kuros-kantoreeyoh-skee
cry	泣く	naku
cubic meter	立方メートル	rippoh mehtoru
cucumber	キュウリ	kyoori
cuddly toy	ぬいぐるみ	nui-gurumi
cuff links	カフス・ボタン	kafs-botan
cup	茶わん	chawan
curly	巻き毛の	maki-ge-no
current	流れ／電流	nagaray/denryuh
cursor	カーソル	cah-soru
cushion	クッション	kusshon
customary	普通／いつも	futsoo/itsumo
customs	税関	zaykan

cut	切る	kiru
cutlery	ナイフとフォークとスプーン	nighf-to fohk-to spoon
cybercafe	インターネットカフェ	intah-netto kafe
cycling	サイクリング	sigh-kuringu

D

dairy products	乳製品	nyoo-say-hin
damage	損害	son-gigh
dance	踊る	odoru
dandruff	ふけ	f-kay
danger	危険	kiken
dangerous	危険な	kiken-na
dark	暗い	ku-righ
date	デート	dayto
daughter (other's)	娘さん	musu-may-san
daughter (own)	娘	musu-may
day	日	hi
day (the whole)	まる一日	maru ichinichi
day before yesterday	一昨日	ototoi
day-trip hot spring	日帰り温泉	higa-eri-onsen
dead	亡くなった	nakunatta
dead zone	デッドゾーン	detto zohn
decaffeinated	カフェインなし／ カフェインフリー	kafayn-nashi/kafayn-free
December	十二月	joo-ni-gats
deck chair	ビーチ・チェアー	beechi-cheyah
declare (customs)	申告する	shin-koku suru
deep	深い	fu-kigh
deep sea diving	スキンダイビング	skin-dighbingu
deep freeze	冷凍庫	raytohko
degrees	度	do
delay	停滞／遅延	tay-tigh/chi-en
delicious	おいしい	o-ishee
dentist	歯医者	ha-isha
dentures	入れ歯	ireba
deodorant	デオドラント	deodoranto
department	部	bu
department store	デパート	depahto
departure	出発	shuppats
departure time	出発時間	shuppats jikan
deposit	手付け金／頭金	te-tsuke-kin/atama-kin
deposit (for safekeeping)	保管	hokan
dessert	デザート	dezahto
destination	行き先	yuki-saki
destination (terminal)	終点	shooten
develop (photo)	現像する	genzoh suru
developer (of software)	（ソフトウェアの）開発者	(sofuto-wea-no) kai- hatsu-sha
diabetic	糖尿病患者	toh-nyoh-byoh kanja
dial	ダイヤル	digh-yaru
diamond	ダイヤモンド	digh-a-mondo
diaper	おしめ	o-shimay
diarrhea	下痢	geri
dictionary	辞典	jiten
diesel/diesel oil	ディーゼル	deezeru
diet	ダイエット	digh-etto
difficulty	困難	kon-nan

digital camera	デジカメ	*deji-kame*
digital single-lens reflex camera	デジタル一眼レフ	*deji-taru ichi-gun-refu*
dining room	食堂	*shoku-doh*
dining/buffet car	食堂車／ビュッフェカー	*shokudoh-sha/buffay-kah*
dinner	ディナー	*dinah*
dinner (to have)	ディナーを食べる	*dinah-o taberu*
direction	方向	*hohkoh*
directly	直接に	*choku-setsu-ni*
dirty	きたない／汚れた	*kita-nigh/yogoreta*
disabled	障害者	*shoh-gigh-sha*
disco	ディスコ	*disko*
discount	割引	*wari-biki*
dish	一皿／一品	*shto-sara/ippin*
dish of the day	今日の料理	*kyoh-no ryohri*
disinfectant	消毒剤	*shohdoku-zigh*
distance	距離	*kyori*
distilled water	蒸留水	*joh-ryoo-swee*
disturb	じゃまする	*jama suru*
disturbance	妨害	*boh-gigh*
dive	潜る	*moguru*
diving	スキンダイビング	*skin-dighbingu*
diving board	飛び込み台	*tobikomi-digh*
diving gear	スキンダイビング・セット	*skin-dighbingu-setto*
divorced	離婚した	*rikon shta*
Do-it-yourself store	日曜大工店	*nichiyoh-dighku-ten*
dizzy	めまい	*me-migh*
do	する	*suru*
doctor	医者	*isha*
dog	犬	*inu*
doll	人形	*nIngyoh*
domestic	国内	*koku-nigh*
done (cooked)	よく料理した	*yoku ryohri shta*
door	戸／ドア	*to/doa*
dot	ドット	*dotto*
double	ダブル	*daburu*
down	下	*shta*
download	ダウンロード	*down-roh-do*
draft (air)	すき間風	*skima-kazay*
dream (verb)	（…を）夢に見る	*(... o) yumay-ni miru*
dress	ドレス	*dores*
dressing gown	部屋着	*heya-gi*
drink (medicine)	薬を飲む	*kusuri-o nomu*
drink (verb)	飲む	*nomu*
drinking water	飲料水	*inryoh-swee*
drive	運転する	*unten suru*
driver	運転手	*untenshu*
driver's licence	運転免許	*unten menkyo*
druggist	薬局	*yakkyoku*
dry	かわいた	*kawa-ita*
dry (verb)	干す	*hosu*
dry clean	ドライクリーニング	*drigh-kreeningu*
dry cleaner's	洗濯屋／クリーニング店	*sentakuya/kreeningu-ten*
during	…中	*... choo*
during (in the middle of)	…の間に	*... no igh-da-ni*
during the day	昼間	*hiruma*

ear	耳	*mimi*
ear, nose and throat specialist	耳鼻・咽喉科	*jibi-inkoh-ka*
earache	耳痛	*jitsoo*
earbud	イヤホン	*ea-hon*
eardrops	耳薬	*mimi-kusuri*
early	早い	*haya-i*
earrings	イヤリング	*iyaringu*
earth	土地	*to-chi*
earthenware	陶器	*toh-ki*
east	東	*higashi*
easy (simple)	簡単な／容易な	*kantan-na/yoh-i-na*
easy (to use)	便利な	*benri-na*
eat	食べる	*taberu*
e-book	電子書籍	*denshi-shoseki/e-bukku*
e-booking/reservations	E-ブッキング	*e-bukking*
eczema	湿疹	*shisshin*
eel	ウナギ	*unagi*
egg	卵	*tamago*
eggplant	ナス	*nasu*
electric	電気（の）	*denki (no)*
electric bicycle	電動自転車	*dendoh jiten sha*
electric car	電気自動車	*denki jidoh sha*
electricity	電気	*denki*
electronics shop	電気屋	*denki ya*
elevator	エレベーター	*ere-baytah*
email	Eメール	*e-may-ru*
embassy	大使館	*tigh-shikan*
emergency brake	緊急ブレーキ	*kinkyoo brayki*
emergency exit	非常口	*hijoh-guchi*
emergency phone	非常電話	*hijoh denwa*
emery board	つめやすり	*tsumay-yasuri*
emperor	天皇	*ten-noh*
empty	からの	*kara-no*
engaged (on the phone)	話し中	*hanashi-choo*
engaged (to be married)	婚約した	*kon-yak-shta*
England	イギリス	*Igirisu*
English (language)	英語	*ay-go*
enjoy	楽しむ	*tano-shimu*
envelope	封筒	*footoh*
e-reader	電子書籍リーダー	*denji-shoseki reader*
escort	コンパニオン	*kompanion*
e-ticket	Eチケット	*e-chiketto*
evening	夕方	*yoo-gata*
evening wear	ディナースーツ／イブニングドレス	*dinah soots (men)/eebu-ningu dores (women)*
event	事件／できごと	*jiken/dekigoto*
everything	全部	*zembu*
everywhere	どこにも	*doko-nimo*
examine	探る	*saguru*
excavation	発掘	*hakkuts*
excellent	優れた	*sugureta*
exchange	交換する	*kohkan suru*
exchange office	為替両替所	*kawase-ryoh-gae-jo*
exchange rate	為替レート	*kawase-rayto*
excursion	遊覧	*yooran*

exhibition	展覧会	tenran-kigh
exit	出口	deguchi
expenses	費用／経費	hiyoh/kayhi
expensive	高い	ta-kigh
explain	説明する	setsumay suru
express	急行電車	kyookoh densha
extension	内線番号	nigh-sen bango
external	外	soto
eye	目	me
eye drops	目薬	me-gusuri
eye shadow	アイシャドー	igh-shadoh
eye specialist	眼科医／目医者	ganka-i/me-isha
eyeliner	アイライナー	igh-righnah

F

face	顔	kao
face-recognition camera	顔認識カメラ	kao nin shiki kamera
factory	工場	koh-joh
fall (verb)	ころぶ	korobu
family	家族	kazoku
famous	有名な	yoo-may-na
far away	遠く	tohku
farm	農家	nohka
farmer	お百姓	ohyakusho
fashion	ファッション	fashon
fast	速い	ha-yigh
father (other's)	お父さま	o-toh-sama
father (own)	父	chichi
fault	誤り	ayamari
fax (verb)	ファックスを送る	fakkusu-o okuru
February	二月	ni-gats
feel	感じる	kanjiru
feel like	好む	konomu
fence	垣根	kaki-ne
ferry	渡し船／フェリーボート	watashi-bunay/feree-bohto
fever	熱	netsu
fill	詰める	tsumeru
fill out	書き込む	kaki-komu
filling	詰め物	tsumemono
film (cinema)	映画	ayga
film (photo)	フィルム	firumu
filter	フィルタ	flrutah
filter cigarette	フィルター付きタバコ	firutah-tski tabako
find	見つける	mitsu-keru
fine (money)	罰金	bakkin
finger	指	yubi
fire	火	hi
fire (on)	火事	kaJl
fire dept.	消防	shoh-boh
fire escape	非常階段	hijoh kigh-dan
fire extinguisher	消火器	shoh-ka-ki
first (in line)	最初に	sigh-sho-ni
first (number one)	第一／一番	dai-ichi/ichiban
first aid	応急手当て	ohkyoo te-atay
first class	一等	ittoh
fish	魚	sakana
fish (verb)	釣をする	tsuri-o suru

fishing rod	釣竿	*tsuri-zao*
fitness club	フィットネスセンター	*fitnes-sentah*
fitness training	フィットネス	*fitnes*
fitting room	試着室	*shichaku-shits*
fix (puncture)	パンクしたタイヤを 直す	*panku shta tigh-ya-o na-osu*
flag	旗	*hata*
flash	フラッシュ	*furash*
flea market	蚤の市	*nomi-no-ichi*
flight	飛行	*hikoh*
flight number	便名	*bin-may*
flood	大水	*ohmizu*
floor	階	*kigh*
flour	粉	*kona*
flu	インフルエンザ	*infruenza*
fly (insect)	ハエ	*ha-e*
fly (verb)	飛ぶ	*tobu*
fog	霧	*kiri*
foggy (to be)	霧がかかる	*kiri-nga kakaru*
folkloristic	民族伝統の	*minzoku dentoh-no*
follow	従う	*shita-ga-u*
food (items)	食品	*shokuhin*
food (stuffs)	食料	*shoku-ryoh*
food poisoning	食中毒	*shoku-choodoku*
foot	足	*ashi*
forbidden	禁止	*kinshi*
forehead	額	*sh-tigh*
foreign	外国の	*gigh-koku-no*
forest bathing	森林浴	*shin-rin-yoku*
forget	忘れる	*wasureru*
fork	フォーク	*fohku*
form	用紙	*yohshi*
forward (a letter)	転送する	*ten-soh suru*
fountain	噴水	*fun-swee*
frame	額縁	*gaku-buchi*
free (no charge)	無料	*muryoh*
free (unoccupied)	空いている	*igh-tay iru*
free time	暇	*hima*
freeze	凍る	*kohru*
French bread	フランスパン	*furansu-pan*
french fries	フライドポテト	*frighdo-poteto*
fresh	新鮮な	*shinsen-na*
Friday	金曜日	*kin-yoh-bi*
fried	焼いた	*yigh-ta*
fried egg	目玉焼き	*medama-yaki*
friend	友達	*tomo-dachi*
friendly	心からの／親切な	*kokoro-kara-no/shinsetu-na*
frightened	恐れる	*osoreru*
fruit	フルーツ／果物	*froots/kudamono*
fruit juice	ジュース	*joosu*
frying pan	フライパン	*furigh-pan*
full (tank)	満タン	*mantan*
fun	楽しい	*tano-shee*

G

gallery	画廊	*garoh*
game	ゲーム	*gaym*
garage (car repair)	修理屋	*shoori-ya*

garbage bag	ごみ袋	*gomi-bukuro*
garden	庭	*niwa*
garden	庭	*niwa*
gas	ガソリン	*gasorin*
gas station	ガソリンスタンド	*gasorin stando*
gear	ギア	*gee-a*
geek	オタク	*otaku*
gel (hair)	ジェル	*jeru*
get married	結婚する	*kekkon suru*
get off	下車する／降りる	*gesha suru/oriru*
gift	贈り物／ギフト	*okuri-mono/gift*
gilt	金メッキ	*kin-mekki*
ginger	ショウガ	*shoh-ga*
girl	女の子	*onna-no ko*
girlfriend	ガールフレンド	*gahru-frendo*
giro check	小切手	*kogittay*
given name	名前	*na-migh*
glass	ガラス	*garas*
glass (drinking)	グラス／コップ	*guras/koppu*
glasses	眼鏡	*me-ganay*
glasses (sun-)	サングラス	*san-guras*
glide	グライダーに乗る	*gu-righdah-ni noru*
glove	手袋	*te-bukuro*
glue	のり	*nori*
gnat (mosquito)	蚊	*ka*
go	行く	*iku*
go back	戻る	*modoru*
go out	外出する	*gigh-shuts suru*
gold	金	*kin*
golf course	ゴルフ場	*gorufu-jo*
good afternoon/day	こんにちは	*kon-nichi-wa*
good evening/night	こんばんは	*komban-wa*
good morning	おはようございます	*ohayoh goza-imas*
good night	おやすみなさい	*oyasumi-na-sigh*
good bye	さようなら	*sayoh-nara*
GPS	ナビ／カーナビ	*nabi/kah-nabi*
grade crossing	踏切	*fumi-kiri*
gram	グラム	*gram*
grandchild	孫	*mago*
grandfather (other's)	おじいさん	*o-jee-san*
grandfather (own)	祖父	*sofu*
grandmother (other's)	お婆さん	*obahsan*
grandmother (own)	祖母	*sobo*
grape juice	グレープ・ジュース	*grayp joosu*
grapefruit	グレープフルーツ	*graypu-furoots*
grapes	ブドウ	*budoh*
grave	墓	*haka*
gray	灰色の／ねずみ色の	*high-iro-no/nezumi-iro-no*
gray (hair)	白髪	*haku-hats*
greasy	脂の多い	*abura-no oh-ee*
green	緑の	*midori-no*
green car	グリーンカー	*green kah*
greet	挨拶する	*igh-sats suru*
grill	網焼きをする／グリルする	*amiyaki-o suru/guriru suru*
grilled	ローストした	*rohst shta*
grocer	食料品店	*shokuryoh-hin-ten*
ground	土地	*tochi*

group	グループ	guroop
guest house	民宿／ペンション	minshuku/penshon
guide (book)	案内書	annigh-sho
guide (person)	ガイド	gigh-do
guided tour	ガイド付きツアー	gigh-do tsuki tsu-ah
gynecologist	産婦人科	san-fujin-ka

H

hacker	ハッカー	hakkah
hair	髪	kami
hairbrush	ヘアブラシ	hea-burashi
hairdresser	床屋／美容院	tokoya/biyoh-in
hairpins	ヘアピン	hea-pin
hairspray	ヘア・スプレー	hea-spray
half	半分	hambun
half full	…を半分	... o hambun
hammer	かなづち	kana-zuchi
hand	手	te
hand brake	ハンド・ブレーキ	hando-burayki
handbag	ハンドバッグ	hando-baggu
handkerchief	ハンカチ	hankachi
handmade	手作り	te-zukuri
happy	嬉しい	ure-shee
harbor	港	minato
hard	堅い	ka-tigh
hash mark	ハッシュマーク／シャープ	hash mah-ku/sharp
hash tag	ハッシュタグ	hush-tagu
hat	帽子	bohshi
hay fever	花粉症	kafun-shoh
head	頭	atama
headache	頭痛	zutsoo
health	健康	kenkoh
health food shop	自然食品店	shizen shoku-hin-ten
hear	聞く	kiku
hearing aid	補聴器	hochoh-ki
heart	心臓	shinzoh
heart patient	心臓病患者	shinzoh-byoh kanja
heat	熱さ	atsusa
heater	ヒーター	heetah
heavy	重い	omo-i
heel	かかと	kakato
hello	こんにちは	kon-nichi-wa
helmet	ヘルメット	herumetto
help	助け	tasukay
help	助ける／手伝う	tas-keru/tetsu-dau
helping (of food)	一人前	shtori-migh
herbal tea	ハーブティー	hahbu-tee
herbs (seasonings)	調味料	chohmi-ryoh
here	ここ	koko
herring	ニシン	nishin
high	高い	ta-kigh
high-definition digital camera	高画質型デジカメ	koh-gashitsu-gata deji-kame
high tide	満潮	manchoh
highchair	子供用椅子	kodomo-yoh isu
highway	高速道路	kosoku doro
hiking	ハイキング	high-kingu

hiking boots	登山靴	*toh-zan-guts*
hip	腰	*koshi*
hire	賃貸する／借りる	*chin-tigh suru/kariru*
hitchhike	ヒッチハイクをする	*hitchi-high-ku-o suru*
hobby	趣味	*shumi*
hold-up	強盗	*gohtoh*
holiday	休暇／休み	*kyooka/yasumi*
holiday (festival)	祭日	*sigh-jits*
holiday (public)	休日	*kyoo-jits*
holiday park	休暇村	*kyoo-ka mura*
holiday rental	別荘	*bessoh*
homesickness	ホームシック	*hohm-shikku*
honest	正直な	*shoh-jiki-na*
honey	蜂蜜	*hachi-mitsu*
horizontal	水平の	*swee-hay-no*
horrible	大変	*tigh-hen*
horse	馬	*uma*
hospital	病院	*byoh-in*
hospitality	もてなし／接待	*mote-nashi/set-tigh*
hot	熱い／暑い	*atsu-i*
hot (bitter, sharp)	辛い	*ka-righ*
hot chocolate	ホットチョコレート	*hotto-choko-rehto*
hotspot	ホットスポット	*hotto spotto*
hot spring	温泉	*onsen*
hotel	ホテル	*hoteru*
hot-water bottle	湯たんぽ	*yoo-tampo*
hour	時間	*jikan*
house	家／うち	*ie/uchi*
household items	家庭用品	*katay yoh-hin*
houses of parliament	国会議事堂	*kok-kigh giji-doh*
housewife	主婦	*shufu*
how far?	どのくらい（遠い）	*dono gurigh (toh-i)*
how long?	どのくらい（長い）	*dono gurigh (na-gigh)*
how much?	いくら	*ikura*
how?	どう	*doh*
hungry (to be)	空腹だ	*koofuku-da*
hurry	急速	*kyoosoku*
husband (other's)	ご主人	*goshujin*
husband (own)	夫／主人	*otto/shujin*
hut	小屋	*koya*
hybrid car	ハイブリットカー	*high-brid kah*

I

ice cubes	氷	*kohri*
ice skate	スケートをする	*skehto-o suru*
ice cream	アイスクリーム	*ighs-kreem*
idea	考え	*kan-ga-e*
identification (card)	身分証明書	*mibun shoh-may-sho*
identify	身分を証明する	*mibun-o shoh-may suru*
ignition key	始動キー	*shidoh kee*
ill	病気	*byoh-ki*
illness	病気	*byoh-ki*
imagine	想像する	*sohzoh suru*
immediately	すぐに	*sugu-ni*
import duty	輸入税	*yunyoo-zay*
impossible	無理な／不可能な	*muri-na/fukanoh-na*
in	…の中に	*....no naka-ni*

in the evening	夕方	*yoogata*
in the morning	午前	*gozen*
included	…を含めて	*.... o fukumete*
included	含めた	*fukumeta*
indicate	示す	*shi-mes*
indicator	方向指示器	*hohkoh-shijiki*
inexpensive	安い	*yasu-i*
infection (viral, bacterial)	伝染（ビールスの、バクテリアの）	*densen (beerus-no, bakuteria-no)*
inflammation	炎症	*enshoh*
information	情報	*joh-hoh*
information (guide)	案内	*an-nigh*
information (material)	資料	*shiryoh*
information office	案内所	*an-nigh-sho*
injection	注射	*choosha*
injured	負傷した	*f-shoh shta*
innocent	無罪な	*mu-zigh-na*
insect	こん虫	*konchoo*
insect bite	虫さされ	*mushi-sasaray*
insect repellent	虫除けクリーム	*mushi-yokay kreem*
inside	中に／内に	*naka-ni/uchi-ni*
insole	靴の内底	*kutsu-no nigh-tay*
instructions	使用法	*shiyoh-hoh*
insurance	保険	*hoken*
intermission	休憩	*kyookay*
international	国際の	*koku-sigh-no*
Internet	インターネット	*intah-netto*
Internet lounge	インターネットラウンジ	*intah-netto raunji*
interpreter	通訳者	*tsooyakusha*
intersection	交差点	*kohsaten*
introduce (oneself)	紹介する	*shoh-kigh suru*
invite	招待する	*shoh-tigh suru*
Ireland	アイルランド	*igh-ru-rando*
iron (clothes)	アイロン	*igh-ron*
iron (metal)	鉄	*tetsu*
iron (verb)	アイロンをかける	*igh-ron-o kakeru*
ironing board	アイロン台	*igh-ron-digh*
island	島	*shima*
itch	かゆい	*kayui*

J

jack	ジャッキ	*jakki*
jacket	ジャケット	*jaketto*
jam	ジャム	*jamu*
January	一月	*ichi-gats*
Japan Rail Pass	JRパス	*JR pas*
Japanese-style bar	居酒屋	*izakaya*
jaw	顎	*ago*
jellyfish	クラゲ	*kuragay*
jeweler	貴金属店／宝石店	*kikinzoku-ten/hohseki-ten*
jewelery	装身具	*soh-shin-gu*
jog	ジョギング	*joggingu*
joke	冗談	*joh-dan*
juice	ジュース	*joosu*
July	七月	*shich-gats*
June	六月	*roku-gats*

K

key	キー／鍵	kee/kagi
key (on keyboard)	キー	key
keyboard	キーボード	key-board
kilo	キロ(グラム)	kiro(gram)
kilometer	キロ(メートル)	kito(mehtoru)
kiss	キス	kisu
kiss (verb)	キスする	kisu suru
kitchen	台所	digh-dokoro
knee	膝	hiza
knee socks	ニー・ソックス／ハイソックス	nee-sokkusu/high-sokkusu
knife	ナイフ	nighfu
knit	編む	amu
know	知る	shiru

L

lace	レース	raysu
lace (shoes)	靴ひも	kutsu-himo
ladies' room	婦人用トイレ	fujinyoh toy-ray
lake	湖	mizu-umi
lamp	ランプ	ramp
land (ground)	土地	tochi
land (verb)	着陸する	chaku riku suru
lane (of traffic)	車線	shasen
language	言葉／言語	kotoba/gengo
laptop computer	ラップトップ	rappu-toppu
large	大きい	ohkee
last	最後／最終	sigh-go/sigh-shoo
last night	昨晩	sakuban
late	遅い	oso-i
later	後程	nochi hodo
laugh	笑う	wara-u
launderette	コインランドリー	koyn randoree
law	法律	hohrits
lawyer	弁護士	ben-goshi
laxative	下剤	ge-zigh
leak (air)	パンク	panku
leather	皮	kawa
leather goods	皮製品	kawa-say-hin
leave	出発する	shuppats suru
leek	長ネギ	naga-negi
left	左	hidari
left (to turn)	左に曲がる	hidari-ni magaru
leg	足	ashi
lemon	レモン	remon
lend	…に貸す	... ni kasu
lens	レンズ	renz
less	少なく	sku-naku
lesson	レッスン	ressun
letter	手紙	tegami
lettuce	レタス	retasu
library	図書館	toshokan
lie	うそ	uso
lie (down)	横になっている	yoko-ni nattay iru
lie (to tell a)	うそをつく	uso-o tsku
lift (hitchhike)	ヒッチハイク	hitchi-high-ku

lift (ski)	リフト	*rifto*
light	ライト	*righ-to*
light (not dark)	明るい	*aka-rui*
light (not heavy)	軽い	*ka-rui*
lighter	ライター	*righ-tah*
lighthouse	灯台	*toh-digh*
lightning	稲妻／稲光／かみなり	*inazuma/ina-bikari/kaminari*
like (verb)	好む／好き	*konomu/ski*
line	線	*sen*
linen	麻／リネン	*asa/rinen*
lipstick	口紅	*kuchi-beni*
liquor store	酒屋	*saka-ya*
liqueur	リキュール	*rikyooru*
listen	聞く	*kiku*
literature	文学	*bun-gaku*
liter	リットル	*rittoru*
little (amount)	少ない	*sku-nigh*
live	住む	*sumu*
lobster	伊勢えび	*isay-ebi*
lock	鍵／錠前	*kagi/johma-e*
log off	ログオフ	*rogu ofu*
log on	ログオン	*rogu on*
log-in page	ログインページ	*rogu-in-pay-ji*
long	長い	*na-gigh*
long distance call	長距離電話	*choh-kyori denwa*
look	見る	*miru*
look for	捜す	*sagasu*
look up	調べる	*shiraberu*
lose (verb)	失う／なくす	*ushina-u/nakusu*
loss	損失	*sonshits*
lost	失った	*ushinatta*
lost (to be)	道に迷う	*michi-ni mayo-u*
lost item	遺失物	*ish-ts-buts*
lost and found office	遺失物取扱所	*ish-ts-buts tori-atsu-kigh-jo*
lotion	ローション	*rohshon*
loud (voice)	大声で	*ohgo-e-de*
love	愛／愛情	*igh/aigh-joh*
love (verb)	愛する	*igh-suru*
love with (to be in)	愛している	*igh-shtay iru*
low	低い	*hiku-i*
low tide	干潮／引き潮	*kanchoh/hiki-shio*
luck	幸運	*koh-un*
luggage	荷物	*nimots*
luggage locker	コイン・ロッカー	*koyn rokkah*
lumps (sugar)	角砂糖	*kaku-zatoh*
lunch	昼食	*choo-shoku*
lunch room (cafe)	コーヒーショップ／喫茶店	*koh-hee-shoppu/kissaten*
lungs	肺	*high*

M

macaroni	マカロニ	*makaroni*
madam	…さん	*...-san*
magazine	雑誌	*zasshi*
maid café	メイドカフェ	*maido-kafe*
mail	郵便	*yoobin*
mailman	郵便屋さん	*yoobin-ya-san*

main post office	郵便局本局／中央郵便局	yoobin-kyoku hon-kyoku/ choo-oh yoobin-kyoku
main road	大通り	ohdohri
make an appointment	約束する	yak-soku suru
make love	セックスする	sekkusu suru
makeshift	一時的な	ichiji-teki-na
malware	マルウェア	maru-wea
man	男	otoko
manager (caretaker)	管理人	kanri-nin
mandarin (fruit)	ミカン	mikan
manicure	マニキュア	manikyua
many	たくさん	tak-san
map	地図	chizu
marble	大理石	digh-ri-seki
March	三月	san-gats
margarine	マーガリン	mahgarin
marina	ヨット用ドック／マリーナ	yotto-yoh dokku/mareena
market	市場／マーケット	ichiba/mahketto
marriage	結婚	kekkon
married	結婚した	kekkon shta
Mass	ミサ	misa
massage	マッサージ	massahji
match	試合	shi-igh
matches	マッチ	matchi
matte (photo)	光沢のない	kohtaku-no nigh
May	五月	go-gats
maybe	多分	tabun
mayonnaise	マヨネーズ	mayonehzu
mayor	市長	shi-choh
meal	食事	shokuji
mean (verb)	意味する	imi suru
meat	肉	niku
medication	薬／薬品	kusuri/yakuhin
medicine	薬品／薬	yakuhin/kusuri
meet	…に会う	… ni au
melon	メロン	meron
melon (water)	西瓜	sweeka
membership (card)	会員証	kigh-in-shoh
menstruate	月経がある	gekkay-ga-aru
menstruation	生理／メンス	sayri/mensu
menu	メニュー／献立	menyoo/kondatay
menu of the day	本日のメニュー	honjitsu no menyoo
message	伝言	dengon
metal	金属	kinzoku
metal detector	金属探知機	kinzoku tanchi ki
meter (in taxi)	メーター	mehtah
meter (100 cm)	メートル	mehtoru
migraine	偏頭痛	henzutsoo
mild (tobacco)	軽い	karui
milk	牛乳／ミルク	gyoo-nyoo/miruku
millimeter	ミリ（メートル）	miri (mehtoru)
mineral water	ミネラルウォーター	mineraru-wohtah
minute	分	fun
mirror	鏡	kagami
miss (a person)	寂しくなる	sabishku-naru
missing (to be)	不足する	fusoku suru
missing person	迷子	migh-go

mistake	間違い	*machi-gigh*
mistaken (to be)	間違える	*machi-ga-eru*
misunderstanding	誤解	*go-kigh*
mixed-baths	混浴	*kon-yoku*
mixture (medicine)	飲み薬	*nomi-gusuri*
mobile banking	モバイルバンキング	*mobairu-bankingu*
mocha	モカ	*moka*
modern art	現代の芸術	*gen-digh-no gay-juts*
molar	奥歯	*okuba*
moment	瞬間	*shunkan*
moment (just a)	ちょっと	*chotto*
monastery	修道院	*shoodoh-in*
Monday	月曜日	*gets-yohbi*
money	お金	*o-kanay*
month	月	*tski*
moped	モペット	*mopetto*
motel	モーテル	*mohteru*
mother (other's)	お母さま	*o-kah-sama*
mother (own)	母	*haha*
motor cross	モトクロス	*moto-kurosu*
motorbike	バイク	*bighk*
motorboat	モーターボート	*mohtah-bohto*
mountain	山	*yama*
mountain climbing	登山	*tozan*
mouse	ネズミ	*nezumi*
mouse (computer's)	マウス	*mausu*
mouth	口	*kuchi*
much	たくさん	*tak-san*
muscle	筋	*suji*
muscle spasms	筋肉けいれん	*kinniku kayren*
museum	美術館／博物館	*bijutsu-kan/hakubutsu-kan*
mushrooms	キノコ	*kinoko*
music	音楽	*on-gaku*
musical	ミュージカル	*myoojikaru*
mussels	イガイ／ムール貝	*i-gigh/mooru-gigh*
mustard	からし／マスタード	*karashi/mastahdo*

N

nail	釘	*kugi*
nail (finger)	つめ	*tsumay*
nail scissors	つめ切り	*tsumay-kiri*
naked	裸／ヌード	*hadaka/noodo*
nationality	国籍	*koku-seki*
natural	自然の	*shizen-no*
nature	自然	*shizen*
naturism	裸体主義	*ra-tigh-shugi*
nauseous	気分が悪い	*kibun-nga waru-i*
near	…の近くに	*... no chikaku-ni*
nearby	ごく近く	*goku-chikaku*
necessary	…が必要	*... nga hitsuyoh*
neck	首	*kubi*
necklace	ネックレス	*nekkuraysu*
needle	針	*hari*
negative (photo)	ネガ	*nega*
neighbors	隣の人	*tonari-no shto*
nephew	甥	*oi*

never	全然…ない／全く…ない	*zenzen ... nigh/mattaku ... nigh*
new	新しい	*atara-shee*
news	ニュース	*nyoos*
news stand	キオスク／売店	*kiosk/biqh-ten*
newspaper	新聞	*shimbun*
next	次の	*tsugi-no*
next to	…のそばに	*... no soba-ni*
nice	楽しい／快適な	*tanoshee/kigh-teki-na*
nice (friendly)	親切	*shin-sets*
nice (happy)	うれしい	*ureshee*
nice (person)	かわいい／よい	*kawa-ee/yoi*
nice (taste)	おいしい	*oi-shee*
niece	姪	*may*
night	夜	*yoru*
night duty	夜勤	*yakin*
nightclub	ナイト・クラブ	*nighto-kurabu*
nipple (bottle)	乳首	*chi-kubi*
no	いいえ	*ii-ye*
no passing	追い越し禁止	*oi-koshi kinshi*
noise	うるさい／騒音	*uru-sigh/soh-on*
non-smoking	禁煙	*kin-en*
nonstop (plane)	直行	*chokkoh*
no one	だれも…ない	*daray-mo ... nigh*
normal	普通	*futsoo*
north	北	*kita*
nose	鼻	*hana*
nose drops	鼻薬	*hana-gusuri*
notepaper	便箋	*binsen*
nothing	何も…ない	*nani-mo ... nigh*
November	十一月	*joo-ichi-gats*
nowhere	どこにも…ない	*doko-nimo ... nigh*
nude beach	ヌーディスト・ビーチ	*noodisto beech*
number	番号	*ban-go*
number plate	ナンバー・プレート	*nanbah-purayto*
nurse	看護婦	*kangofu*
nuts	ナッツ／おつまみ	*nattsu/otsumami*

O

October	十月	*joo-gats*
off (gone bad)	くさった	*kusatta*
offer	申し出る	*mohshi deru*
office	事務所／オフィス	*jimusho/ofiss*
oil	油／オイル	*abura/oiru*
oil level	オイルの量	*oiru-no ryoh*
ointment	軟膏	*nankoh*
ointment for burns	火傷の軟膏	*yakedo-no nanko*
okay	OK	*OK*
old (thing/person)	古い／年とった	*furui/toshi-totta*
olive oil	オリーブ油	*oreebu-yoo*
olives	オリーブ	*oreebu*
omelette	オムレツ	*omurets*
on	…の上に	*... no ue-ni*
on board (to go)	乗船する	*johsen suru*
on the right	右の方に	*migi-no hoh-ni*
on the way	途中で	*tochoo-de*
oncoming car	対向車	*tigh-koh-sha*

one-way traffic	一方通行	*ippoh tsookoh*
onion	玉ねぎ	*tama-negi*
open (to be)	開いている	*ightay-iru*
open (verb)	開ける	*akeru*
open-air bath	露天風呂	*roten-buro*
opera	オペラ	*opera*
operate (surgeon)	手術する	*shujuts suru*
operator (telephone)	交換手	*kohkanshu*
opposite	向こう側	*mukoh-gawa*
optician	眼鏡屋	*megane-ya*
orange	オレンジ	*orenji*
orange (color)	オレンジ色	*orenji-iro*
orange juice	オレンジ・ジュース	*orenji-joosu*
order	注文	*choomon*
order (tidy)	片づいた	*kata-zuita*
order (verb)	注文する	*choomon suru*
otaku shop	オタクショップ	*otaku-shoppu*
other	他の	*hoka-no*
other side	向こう側	*mukoh-gawa*
outside	外	*soto*
overpass	高架橋	*kohka-kyoh*
over there	あそこ	*asoko*
overtake	追い越す	*oi-kosu*
oysters	カキ	*kaki*

P

pacemaker	ペースメーカー	*pe-su me-kah*
packed lunch	弁当	*bentoh*
page	ページ	*payji*
pain	痛み	*itami*
painkiller	痛み止め／鎮痛剤	*itami-domay/chin-tsoo-zigh*
paint	ペンキ	*penki*
painting	絵画	*kigh-ga*
pajamas	パジャマ	*pajyama*
palace	宮殿／皇居	*kyooden/kohkyo*
pan	鍋	*nabay*
pancake	パンケーキ	*pan-kehki*
pancake (Japanese style)	ホットケーキ	*hotto-kehki*
pane	窓ガラス	*mado-garas*
pants	ズボン／スラックス	*zubon/surakks*
paper	紙	*kami*
parasol	日傘	*higasa*
parcel	小包み	*ko-zutsu-mi*
pardon	すみません	*sumimasen*
parents (other's)	ご両親	*go-ryohshin*
parents (own)	両親	*ryohshin*
park	公園	*koh-en*
park (verb)	駐車する	*choosha suru*
parking garage	駐車場	*choosha-jo*
parking space (meter)	駐車メーター	*choosha mehtah*
parsley	パセリ	*paseri*
part (car-)	部品	*buhin*
partner	恋人	*koi-bito*
party	パーティー	*pahtay*
passable (road)	通行出来る	*tsoo-koh dekiru*
passenger	旅客	*ryokyaku*
passport	パスポート	*pasupohto*

passport photo	証明写真	*shoh-may shashin*
password	パスワード	*pasu-wahdo*
patient	病人	*byohnin*
pavement	歩道	*hodoh*
pay	払う	*hara-u*
pay the bill	勘定を払う	*kanjoh-o hara-u*
peach	桃	*momo*
peanuts	ピーナッツ	*peenattsu*
pear	梨	*nashi*
peas	グリーンピース	*gureenpeesu*
pedal	ペダル	*pedaru*
pedestrian crossing	横断歩道	*ohdan-hodoh*
pedicure	ペディキュア	*pedikyua*
pen	ペン	*pen*
pencil	鉛筆	*empits*
pepper	胡椒	*koshoh*
performance	上演	*joh-en*
perfume	香水	*kohswe*
perm (hair)	パーマ（ネント）	*pahma (nento)*
perm (verb)	パーマをかける	*pahma-o kakeru*
permit	許可書	*kyoka-sho*
person	…人	*…-nin*
personal	個人的	*kojinteki*
pets	ペット	*petto*
pharmacy	薬局	*yak-kyok*
phone (tele-)	電話	*denwa*
phone (verb)	電話をかける	*denwa-o kakeru*
phone booth	電話ボックス	*denwa bokkusu*
phone directory	電話帳	*denwa-choh*
photo-editing	画像処理	*gazoh shori*
phone number	電話番号	*denwa-ban-goh*
photo	写真	*shashin*
photocopier	コピーマシン	*kopee-mashin*
photocopy	コピー	*kopee*
photocopy (verb)	コピーする	*kopee suru*
pick up (come to)	取りに来る	*tori-ni kuru*
pick up (go to)	取って来る	*tottay kuru*
picnic	ピクニック	*pikunikku*
pier	埠頭	*f-toh*
pigeon	ハト	*hato*
pill (contraceptive)	避妊薬／ピル	*hi-nin-yaku/piru*
pillow	枕	*makura*
pillowcase	枕カバー	*makura-kabah*
pin	ピン／留め針	*pin/tomebari*
PIN number	暗証番号	*ansho-bango*
pineapple	パイナップル	*pighn-appuru*
pipe	パイプ	*pighpu*
pipe tobacco	パイプ用たばこ	*pighpu-yoh tabako*
pity	残念	*zannen*
pixel	画素	*gaso*
place of interest	みどころ／観光地	*midokoro/kankoh-chi*
plan	計画	*kay-kaku*
plant	植物	*shokubuts*
plastic	プラスチック	*puraschik*
plastic bag	ビニール袋	*bineeru-bukuro*
plate	皿	*sara*
platform	（プラット）ホーム	*(puratto) hohmu*

play	劇	geki
play (verb)	遊ぶ	asobu
play golf	ゴルフをする	gorufu-o suru
play sports	スポーツをする	spohts-o suru
play tennis	テニスをする	tenisu-o suru
playground	遊園地	yoo-en-chi
playing cards	トランプ	torampu
pleasant	気持ちのよい	kimochi-no-yoi
please	お願いします	o-ne-gigh-shimas
pleasure	楽しみ	tano-shimi
plum	梅	umay
pocketknife	ポケットナイフ	poketto-nighfu
point	指さす	yubi sasu
poison	毒	doku
police	警察	kay-sats
police station	警察署／交番	kay-satsu-sho/kohban
policeman	警察官／おまわりさん	kaysats-kan/omawari-san
pond	池	ikay
pony	ポニー馬	ponee-uma
population	人口	jinkoh
pork	豚肉	buta-niku
port	ポートワイン	pohto-wighn
porter	赤帽	akaboh
porter (concierge)	門番／守衛	momban/shu-ay
post (zip) code	郵便番号	yoobin ban-go
post office	郵便局	yoobin-kyoku
postage	郵便料金	yoobin ryohkin
postbox	ポスト／郵便箱	posto /yoobin bako
postcard	葉書／絵葉書	hagaki/e-hagaki
postman	郵便屋さん	yoobin-ya-san
potato	ジャガイモ	jaga-imo
potato chips	ポテトチップ	poteto-chippu
poultry	家禽	kakin
powdered milk	粉ミルク	kona-miruku
power outlet	コンセント	konsento
power spots	パワースポット	pawah-supotto
prawns	小エビ	ko-ebi
precious	貴重	kichoh
prefer	…方が好きだ	... hoh-nga ski da
preference	好み	konomi
pregnant	妊娠	nin-shin
prescription	処方	shohoh
present (not absent)	出席	shus-seki
present (gift)	プレゼント	purezento
press	押す	osu
pressure	圧力	atsu-ryoku
price	値段	nedan
price list	値段表	nedan-hyoh
print	プリント	printo
print (verb)	プリントする	printo suru
prior seats	優先席	you-sen seki
probably	多分	tabun
problem	問題	mon-digh
profession	職業	shoku-gyoh
program	プログラム	program
pronounce	発音する	hatsuon suru
pudding (caramel)	プディング／プリン	pudingu/purin

pull	引く	*hiku*
pull a muscle	筋肉を痛める	*kin-niku-o itameru*
pulse	脈	*myaku*
pure	純粋な	*junswee-na*
purple	紫色	*murasaki-iro*
purse	ハンドバッグ	*hando-baggu*
purse (money)	サイフ	*sigh-f*
push	押す	*osu*
puzzle	なぞ／パズル	*nazo/pazuru*

Q

quarter	四分の一	*yombun-no ichi*
quarter of an hour	十五分	*joo-gofun*
queen	女王	*jo-oh*
question	質問	*shitsumon*
quick	速く	*hayaku*
quiet	静かな	*shizuka-na*

R

radio	ラジオ	*rajio*
railways	鉄道	*tetsudoh*
rain	雨	*amay*
rain (verb)	雨が降る	*amay-ga furu*
raincoat	レインコート	*rayn kohto*
rape	強姦	*gohkan*
rapids	急流	*kyooryoo*
raw	生の	*nama-no*
raw ham	生ハム	*nama-hamu*
raw vegetables	生の野菜	*nama-no ya-sigh*
razor blades	かみそり	*kamisori*
read	読む	*yomu*
ready	用意の出来た	*yoh-i-no dekita*
really	ほんとうに	*hontoh-ni*
receipt	領収書／受取書	*ryoh-shuh-sho/uketorisho*
recipe	料理法	*ryohri-hoh*
reclining chair	リクライニング・チェア	*rikrighning chea*
recommend	推薦する	*sweesen suru*
rectangle	長方形	*choh-hoh-kay*
red	赤い	*a-kigh*
red wine	赤ワイン	*aka-wighn*
reduction	減少	*genshoh*
refrigerator	冷蔵庫	*rayzoh-ko*
regards	…によろしく	*... ni yoroshku*
region	地方	*chihoh*
registered	書留	*kaki-tomay*
regular (gasoline)	レギュラー	*regurah*
relatives	家族	*kazoku*
reliable	確かな	*tash-ka-na*
religion	宗教	*shoo-kyoh*
rent out	賃貸する	*chin-tigh suru*
repair	修理をする	*shoori-o suru*
repairs	修理	*shoori*
repeat	繰り返す	*kuri-ka-esu*
report (police)	調書	*choh-sho*
reserve	予約する	*yoyaku suru*
responsible	責任がある	*sekinin-ga aru*
rest	休憩する／休む	*kyookay suru/yasumu*

restaurant	レストラン	resutoran
result	結果	kekka
retired	退職した	tigh-shoku shta
return (ticket)	往復(切符)	ohf-ku (kippu)
reverse (vehicle)	バックする	bakk suru
rheumatism	リューマチ	ryoomachi
rice (cooked)	ごはん	gohan
rice (grain)	米	komay
ridiculous	ばかな／よしたまえ	baka-na/yoshi-tama-e
riding (horseback)	乗馬	johba
riding school	乗馬学校	johba gakkoh
right	右	migi
right of way	優先	yoosen
ripe	熟した	juku shta
risk	危険	kiken
river	川	kawa
road	道路	dohro
roadway	自動車道	jidohsha-doh
rock	岩	iwa
roll	ロールパン	rohru-pan
roof rack	ルーフ・ラック	roof-rakku
room	部屋	he-ya
room number	部屋番号	he-ya ban-go
room service	ルーム・サービス	room sahbis
rope	紐／ロープ	himo/rohp
ros (wine)	ロゼ	rozay
route	道	michi
rowing boat	ボート	bohto
rubber	ゴム	gomu
rubber band	ゴム輪	gomu-wa
rude	失礼な	shits-ray-na
ruins	廃虚	high-kyo
run into	…に出会う	... ni de-au
running shoes	スポーツ・シューズ	spohts-shooz

s

sad	悲しい	kana-shee
safe (adj.)	安全な	anzen-na
safe	金庫	kinko
safety pin	安全ピン	anzen-pin
sail (verb)	ヨットを走らせる	yotto-o hashiraseru
sailing boat	ヨット	yotto
salad	サラダ	sarada
salad oil	サラダ油	sarada-yoo
salami	サラミソーセージ	sarami sohsehji
sale	売り出し	uridashi
salt	塩	shio
same	同じ	onaji
sandy beach	砂浜	suna-hama
sanitary pad	生理用ナプキン	sayri-yoh napkin
sardines	イワシ	iwashi
satisfied	満足した	manzoku shta
Saturday	土曜日	do-yoh-bi
sauce	ソース	sohsu
sauna	サウナ	sauna
sausage	ソーセージ	sohsehji
say	言う	yoo

scanner	スキャナー	*sukyanah*
scarf	スカーフ／マフラー	*skahf/mafurah*
scenic walk	散歩道	*sampo-michi*
school	学校	*gakkoh*
scissors	はさみ	*hasami*
scooter	スクーター	*skootah*
Scotch tape	セロテープ	*serotehpu*
Scotland	スコットランド	*Skottorando*
scrambled eggs	煎り卵	*iri-tamago*
screen	スクリーン	*suku-reen*
screw	ねじ	*neji*
screwdriver	ねじ回し／ドライバー	*neji-mawashi/dorighbah*
sculpture	彫刻	*choh-kok*
SD card	SDカード	*SD kah-do*
sea	海	*umi*
search engine	サーチエンジン	*sah-chi enjin*
seasick	船酔い	*funa-yoi*
seat	座席	*zaseki*
second	秒	*byoh*
second (in line)	第二	*digh-ni*
second-hand	中古品	*chooko-hin*
security	セキュリティー	*sekyuritea*
sedative	鎮静剤	*chinsay-zigh*
see	見る	*miru*
see (go sightseeing)	観光に行く	*kankoh-ni iku*
self-catering accommodation	素泊まり	*sudomari*
self-timer	セルフ・タイマー	*serufu-tighmah*
send	送る	*okuru*
sentence	文章	*bunshoh*
September	九月	*ku-gats*
serious	深刻な	*shinkoku-na*
service	サービス	*sahbis*
serviette	ナプキン	*napukin*
set	セット	*setto*
sewing needs	裁縫道具	*sigh-hoh dohgu*
shade	陰	*kagay*
shallow	浅い	*a-sigh*
shammy (chamois)	セーム皮	*sehmu-gawa*
shampoo	シャンプー	*shampoo*
shark	サメ／フカ	*samay/f-ka*
shave	剃る	*soru*
shaver	シェーバー／電気かみそり	*shaybah/denki kamisori*
shaving brush	ひげ剃り用ブラシ	*hige-sori-yoh burashi*
shaving cream	シェービング・クリーム	*shaybingu-kureemu*
shaving soap	ひげ剃り用石けん	*hige-sori-yoh sekken*
sheet	シーツ	*sheets*
sherry	シェリー	*she-ree*
shirt	シャツ	*shats*
shoe	靴	*ku-tsu*
shoe polish	靴クリーム	*kutsu-kureemu*
shoe shop	靴屋	*ku-tsu-ya*
shoemaker	靴直し	*kutsu-naoshi*
shop	店	*misay*
shop (verb)	買い物をする	*kigh-mono-o suru*
shop assistant	販売員／店員	*han-bigh-in/ten-in*
shop window	ショーウィンドー	*shoh-windoh*

shopping center	ショッピングセンター	shoppingu-sentah
short	短い	miji-kigh
short circuit	ショート	shohto
shorts	半ズボン	han-zubon
shoulder	肩	kata
show	ショー／上演	shoh/joh-en
shower	シャワー	shawah
shutter	シャッター	shattah
sieve	ふるい	furui
sign (name)	署名する	shomay suru
sign (road)	交通標識	kohtsoo hyoh-shiki
signal/reception for cell phone	電場	denpa
signature	署名／サイン	sho-may/sign
silence	沈黙／静けさ	chinmoku/shizukesa
silver	銀	gin
SIM card	SIMカード	shimu kah-do
simple	単純な	tanjun-na
single	シングル	shinguru
single (one way)	片道	katamichi
single (unmarried)	独身の	dokushin-no
single-lens reflex (SLR) camera	一眼レフカメラ	ichi-gun-refu kamera
sir	…さん	...-san
sister (elder, other's)	お姉さん	o-nay-san
sister (elder, own))	姉	anay
sister (younger, other's)	妹さん	imohto-san
sister (younger, own)	妹	imohto
sit	座る	suwaru
size	サイズ	sighzu
ski	スキーする	skee suru
ski boots	スキー靴	skee-gutsu
ski goggles	スキー用ゴーグル	skee-yoh gohguru
ski instructor	スキー指導員	skee shidoh-in
ski lessons/class	スキーレッスン／教室	skee ressun/kyoh-shtsu
ski lift	スキーリフト	skee-rifuto
ski pants	スキーズボン／スキー用パンツ	skee-zubon/skee-yoh pants
ski pole	ストック	stokku
ski slope	ゲレンデ	gerenday
ski suit	スキースーツ	skee-soots
ski wax	スキー用ワックス	skee-yoh wakkusu
skin	肌	hada
skirt	スカート	sukahto
skis	スキー	skee
sleep	眠る	nemuru
sleeping car	寝台車	shin-digh-sha
sleeping pills	睡眠薬	sui-min-yaku
slide	スライド	su-righdo
slip	シミーズ／ペティコート	shimeez/petikohto
slow	ゆっくり	yukkuri
slow train	各駅列車	kaku-eki ressha
small	小さい	chee-sigh
small change	小銭	kozeni
smart phone	スマートフォン／スマホ	sumah-to fon/sumaho
smell	臭う	ni-ou
smoke	煙	kemuri

smoked	薫製した	*kunsay shta*
smoking	喫煙	*kitsu-en*
smoking compartment	喫煙車	*kitsu-en-sha*
snake	ヘビ	*hebi*
snorkel	スノーケル	*snohkeru*
snow	雪	*yuki*
snow (verb)	雪が降る	*yuki-ga furu*
snowboarding	スノーボード／スノボ	*sunoh/boh-do/sunobo*
snow chains	チェーン	*chayn*
soap	石けん	*sekken*
soap box	石けん箱	*sekken-bako*
soap powder	粉石けん	*kona-sekken*
soccer	サッカー	*sakkah*
soccer match	サッカー試合	*sakkah-ji-igh*
social networking	ソーシャルネットワーキング	*soh-sharu netto wah-kingu*
socket	コンセント	*konsento*
socks	靴下／ソックス	*kutsu-shta/sokkusu*
soft drink	ソフト・ドリンク	*sofut-dorinku*
software	ソフトウェア	*sofuto-wea*
sole (fish)	舌びらめ	*shta-biramay*
sole (shoe)	靴底	*kutsu-soko*
someone	誰か	*daray-ka*
sometimes	時々	*toki-doki*
somewhere	どこか	*doko-ka*
son (other's)	息子さん	*mus-ko-san*
son (own)	息子	*mus-ko*
soon	早く	*hayaku*
sore	傷	*kizu*
sore throat	のどの痛み	*nodo-no itami*
sorry	すみません	*sumimasen*
soup	スープ	*soop*
sour	すっぱい	*sup-pigh*
sour cream	サワークリーム	*sawah-kureemu*
south	南	*minami*
souvenir	おみやげ／おみやげ品	*omiyagay/omiyage-hin*
soy sauce	醤油	*shoh-yu*
spaghetti	スパゲッティ	*spagetti*
spare	予備	*yobi*
spare parts	予備部品	*yobi-buhin*
speak	話す	*hanasu*
special	特別な	*tokubets-na*
specialist (doctor)	専門医	*semmon-i*
speciality (cooking)	特別料理	*tokubets ryohri*
speed limit	最高速度	*sigh-koh sokudo*
spell	つづる	*tsuzuru*
spicy	スパイシー	*spighshee*
splinter	とげ	*togay*
spoon	スプーン	*spoon*
sport	スポーツ	*spohtsu*
sports center	スポーツ・センター	*spohts-sentah*
spot (place)	場所	*basho*
sprain	くじく	*kujiku*
spring	春	*haru*
square (plaza)	広場	*hiroba*
square (shape)	正方形	*sayhoh-kay*
square meters	平方メートル	*hayhoh mehtoru*
squash	スカッシュをする	*skahsh-o suru*

stadium	スタジアム	*stajiam*
stain	しみ	*shimi*
stain remover	しみ取り	*shimi-tori*
stairs	階段	*kigh-dan*
stamp	切手	*kittay*
start	動き出させる	*ugoki-dasaseru*
station	駅	*eki*
statue	像	*zoh*
stay (in hotel)	宿泊する	*shuku-haku suru*
stay (remain)	滞在	*tigh-zigh*
steal	盗む	*nusumu*
steel	鋼鉄	*kohtets*
stench	臭いにおい	*ku-sigh ni-oi*
sting (noun)	虫さされ	*mushi-sasaray*
stitch (med.)	（傷を）縫い合わせる	*(kizu-o) nui-awaseru*
stitch (verb)	縫う	*noo*
stock (soup)	スープの素	*soop-no moto*
stockings	ストッキング	*stokkingu*
stomach	胃	*i*
stomach (abdominal region)	腹／腹部	*hara/fukubu*
stomach ache	腹痛	*fuku-tsoo*
stomach cramps	激しい腹痛	*hageshee fuku-tsoo*
stools	糞便	*fumben*
stop	止まる	*tomaru*
stop (bus)	停留所／停車場	*tay-ryoo-jo/tay-sha-jo*
stopover	途中下車	*tochoo-gesha*
storm	嵐	*arashi*
straight	真っ直ぐ	*massugu*
straight ahead	真っ直ぐに	*massugu-ni*
straw	ストロー	*sutoroh*
strawberries	イチゴ	*ichigo*
street	道	*michi*
street side	道端	*michibata*
strike	スト（ライキ）	*suto (righki)*
strong	強い	*tsuyo-i*
study	勉強する	*benkyoh suru*
stuffing	詰め物	*ts-me-mono*
subtitled	字幕付きで	*jimaki-tski-de*
subway	地下	*chika*
subway station	地下鉄の駅	*chikatetsu-no eki*
subway system	地下鉄	*chikatetu*
succeed	出来る	*dekiru*
sugar	砂糖	*satoh*
suit	スーツ	*soots*
suitcase	スーツケース	*soots-kays*
summer	夏	*nats*
sun	太陽	*tigh-yoh*
sun hat	日よけ帽	*hiyoke-boh*
sunbathe	日光浴	*nikkoh-yoku*
Sunday	日曜日	*nichi-yoh-bi*
sunglasses	サングラス	*san-guras*
sunrise	日の出	*hinoday*
sunset	日暮れ	*higuray*
sunstroke	日射病	*nissha-byoh*
suntan lotion	日焼け止めクリーム	*hiyakedome kureemu*
suntan oil	日焼けオイル	*hiyake-oiru*

supermarket	スーパー（マーケット）	*soopah (mahketto)*
surcharge	追加料金	*tsuika ryohkin*
surf	サーフィンをする	*sahfin-o suru*
surf board	サーフボード	*sahfu-bohdo*
surname	苗字	*myoh-ji*
surprise	驚き	*odoroki*
swallow	飲みこむ	*nomi-komu*
swamp	沼地	*numa-chi*
sweat	汗	*asay*
sweater	セーター	*sehtah*
sweet	甘い	*ama-i*
sweet (kind)	親切な	*shin-sets-na*
sweet corn	トウモロコシ	*toh-moro-koshi*
swim	泳ぐ	*oyogu*
swimming pool	プール	*pooru*
swimming trunks	水泳パンツ	*swee-ay pants*
swindle	詐欺	*sagi*
switch	スイッチ	*switchi*
synagogue	ユダヤ教の会堂	*yudayakyoh-no kigh-doh*
syrup	シロップ	*shiroppu*

T

table	テーブル	*tehburu*
table tennis	卓球／ピンポン	*takkyoo/pin-pon*
tablet	錠剤	*joh-zigh*
tablet PC	タブレット型パソコン	*taburetto-gata paso-kon*
take (medicine)	服用する	*fukuyoh suru*
take (photograph)	（写真を）撮る	*(shashin-o) toru*
take (time)	時間がかかる	*jikan-nga kakaru*
talcum powder	タルカム・パウダー	*tarukamu paudah*
talk	話す	*hanasu*
tall	背が高い	*say-nga ta-kigh*
tampons	タンポン	*tampon*
tanned	日に焼けた	*hi-ni yaketa*
tap	蛇口	*jaguchi*
tap water	水道の水	*sweedoh-no mizu*
taste (verb)	試す	*tamesu*
taste	味	*aji*
tax free shop	免税店	*menzay-ten*
taxi	タクシー	*takshee*
taxi stand	タクシー乗り場	*takshee noriba*
tea	お茶	*ocha*
tea (black)	紅茶	*kohcha*
tea (green)	緑茶	*ryokucha*
tea ceremony	お茶会	*ocha-kigh*
teapot	急須／ティーポット	*kyoosu/tee-pott*
teaspoon	茶さじ／ティースプーン	*chasaji/tee-spoon*
telegram	電報	*dempoh*
telephoto lens	望遠レンズ	*boh-en renzu*
television	テレビ	*terebi*
telex	テレックス	*terekkusu*
temperature (body)	体温	*tigh-on*
temperature (heat)	温度	*ondo*
temperature (weather)	気温	*kion*
temporary filling	一時的な虫歯の詰め物	*ichiji-teki-na mushiba-no tsumemono*
tender	柔らかい	*yawara-kigh*

tennis ball	テニスボール	tenisu-bohru
tennis court	テニスコート	tenisu-kohto
tennis racket	テニスラケット	tenisu-raketto
tent	テント	tento
tent peg	ペグ	pegu
terrace	テラス	terasu
terribly	大変な	tigh-hen-na
texting	メール	may-ru
thank	お礼を言う	oray-o yoo
thank you	ありがとうございます	arigatoh go-zigh-mas
thanks	ありがとう	arigatoh
thaw	溶ける	tokeru
the day after tomorrow	あさって	asattay
theatre	劇場	gekijo
theft	窃盗	settoh
there	そこ	soko
thermal bath	温泉	onsen
thermometer (body)	体温計	tigh-onkay
thermometer (weather)	温度計	ondokay
thick	太い	f-toy
thief	泥棒	doroboh
thigh	太腿	fto-momo
thin (not fat)	細い／痩せた	hoso-i/yaseta
thin (not thick)	薄い	usu-i
think	思う	omo-u
think (consider)	考える	kanga-eru
third (¹/₃)	三分の一	sambun no ichi
thirsty (to be)	のどが渇く	nodo-ga kawaku
this afternoon	今日の午後	kyoh-no gogo
this evening	今晩	komban
this morning	今日の午前	kyoh-no gozen
thread	糸	ito
throat	喉	nodo
throat lozenges	せき止めドロップ	seki-domay doroppu
throw up	吐く	haku
thunderstorm	雷雨	righ-u
Thursday	木曜日	moku-yohbi
ticket	切符	kippu
ticket office (travel)	みどりの窓口	midori-no mado-guchi
ticket (admission)	入場券	nyoo-joh-ken
ticket (travel)	切符	kippu
tickets (seat)	座席券	zaseki-ken
tidy	片付ける	kata-zukeru
tie	ネクタイ	neku-tigh
tights	パンスト	pan-sto
time	時間	jikan
times	回	kigh
timetable	時刻表	jikoku-hyoh
tin (canned)	缶詰め	kanzu-may
tip	チップ	chippu
tire	タイヤ	tigh-ya
tire pressure	タイヤ圧力ティッシュペーパー	tigh-ya atsu-ryoku tissues tisshoo-pehpah
toast	トースト	tohsto
tobacco	たばこ	tabako
toboggan	そり	sori
today	今日	kyoh

toe	足の指	*ashi-no yubi*
together	一緒に	*issho-ni*
toilet	トイレ／お手洗い／便所	*toiray/o-te-a-righ/benjo*
toilet paper	トイレットペーパー	*toiretto-pehpah*
toiletries	化粧品	*keshoh-hin*
tomato	トマト	*tomato*
tomato puree	トマトピューレー	*tomato-pyooray*
tomato sauce	トマトケチャップ	*tomato-kechappu*
tomorrow	明日	*ashta*
tongue	舌	*shta*
tonight	今晩／今夜	*komban/konya*
tools	道具	*doh-gu*
tooth	歯	*ha*
toothache	歯痛	*ha-ita*
toothbrush	歯ブラシ	*ha-burashi*
toothpaste	歯磨	*ha-migaki*
toothpick	ようじ	*yohji*
top up	おかわり	*okawari*
total	全部	*zen-bu*
tough	固い	*ka-tigh*
tour	ツアー／周遊／旅行	*tsu-ah/shoo-yoo/ryokoh*
tour guide	案内者／ガイド	*an-nigh-sha/gighdo*
tourist class	二等	*nitoh*
Tourist Information office	観光案内所	*kankoh an-nigh-sho*
tow	牽引する	*ken-in suru*
tow cable	牽引ロープ	*ken-in rohpu*
towel	タオル／手拭い	*ta-oru/te-nugui*
tower	塔	*toh*
town	町	*machi*
town hall	市役所	*shiyakusho*
toys	おもちゃ	*omocha*
traffic	交通	*kohtsoo*
traffic light	信号	*shingo*
train	列車	*ressha*
train (electric)	電車	*densha*
train ticket	切符	*kippu*
train timetable	時刻表	*jikoku-hyoh*
translate	翻訳する	*hon-yaku suru*
travel	旅行する	*ryokoh suru*
travel agent	旅行代理店	*ryokoh-dighri-ten*
travel guide	旅行案内／案内書	*ryokoh an-nigh/ an-nigh-sho*
traveler	旅行者	*ryokohsha*
traveler's check	旅行用小切手	*ryokoh-yoh kogittay*
treatment	治療	*chi-ryoh*
triangle	三角	*sankaku*
trim	切りそろえる	*kiri-soro-eru*
trip	旅行	*ryokoh*
trip (sightseeing)	観光	*kankoh*
trip (walk)	散歩	*sampo*
trout	マス（鱒）	*masu*
truck	トラック	*trakku*
trustworthy	たよりになる	*tayori-ni naru*
try on	試着する	*shichaku suru*
tube	チューブ	*choob*
Tuesday	火曜日	*ka-yohbi*

tuna	マグロ	maguro
tunnel	トンネル	tonneru
turn	回	kigh
TV	テレビ	terebi
TV guide	テレビガイド	terebi gigh-do
tweet	ツイート／つぶやき	tsu-e-to/tsubuyaki
tweezers	ピンセット	pinsetto
typhoon	台風	tigh-foo

U

ugly	みにくい／美しくない	minikui/utsu-kushiku-nigh
umbrella	傘	kasa
under	…の下に	... no shta-ni
underpants	パンツ	pants
understand	分かる／理解する	wakaru/ri-kigh suru
underwear	下着	shta-gi
undress	服を脱ぐ	fuku-o nugu
unemployed	失業	shits-gyoh
uneven (ground)	でこぼこの	dekoboko-no
university	大学	digh-gaku
unleaded	無鉛／レギュラーガソリン	mu-en/regyurah-gasorin
up	上	ue
upload	アップロード	up-roh-do
urgent	非常／緊急	hijoh/kinkyoo
urgently	早急に	sohkyoo-ni
urine	小便／おしっこ	shohben/oshikko
used bookstore	古本屋	furu-hon ya
username	ユーザー名	you-zah-may
usually	たいてい	tigh-tay

V

vacate	立ち退く	tachi-noku
vaccinate	予防接種	yoboh sesshu
vagina	膣	chitsu
valid	価値のある	kachi-no aru
valley	谷	tani
valuable	高価な	kohka-na
van	中型ヴァン／ミニバス	choogata-van/minibas
vanilla	バニラ	banira
vase	花瓶	kabin
veal	小牛の肉	ko-ushi-no niku
vegetable soup	野菜スープ	ya-sigh soop
vegetables	野菜	ya-sigh
vegetarian	ベジタリアン／菜食家	bejitarian/sigh-shokka
vein	静脈	joh-myaku
vending machine	自動販売機	jidoh ham-bigh-ki
venereal disease	性病	say-byoh
via	経由	kay-yoo
video	動画	doh-ga
video camera	ビデオ・カメラ	bideo-kamera
video recorder	ビデオレコーダー	bideo-rekohdah
video tape	ビデオテープ	bideo-tehpu
view	眺め	nagamay
village	村	mura
virus	ウィルス	oui-rusu
visa	ビザ	biza
visit	訪問する	hohmon suru

190

visiting card	名刺	*mayshi*
visiting time	面会時間	*menkigh jikan*
vitamin tablets	ビタミン剤	*bitamin-zigh*
vitamins	ビタミン	*bitamin*
volcano	火山	*kazan*
volleyball	バレーボール	*baray-bohru*
vomit	吐く／戻す	*haku/modosu*

W

wait	待つ	*matsu*
waiter	ウェーター	*waytah*
waiting room	待合室	*machi-a-i-shitsu*
waitress	ウェイトレス	*waytresu*
wake up	起きる	*okiru*
Wales	ウェールズ	*wayruzu*
walk (noun)	散歩	*sampo*
walk (verb)	散歩する／歩く	*sampo suru/aruku*
wallet	財布	*sighfu*
warm	温かい	*atatakigh*
warn	注意する	*choo-i suru*
warning	注意	*choo-i*
wash	洗う	*ara-u*
washing	洗濯物	*sentaku-mono*
washing machine	洗濯機	*sentakki*
wasp	スズメバチ	*suzume-bachi*
watch	腕時計	*uday-do-kay*
water	水	*mizu*
water ski	水上スキーをする	*sweejoh skee-o suru*
watermill	水車	*sweesha*
waterproof	防水	*bohswee*
wave-pool	人工波プール／波のある プール	*jinkoh-ha pooru/nami-no aru pooru*
way (direction)	方面	*hohmen*
way (method)	手段／方法	*shudan/hoh-hoh*
we	私達	*watash-tachi*
weak	弱い	*yowa-i*
weather	天気	*tenki*
weather forecast	天気予報	*tenki yo-hoh*
Web site	ウェブサイト	*webu-sight*
wedding	結婚式	*kekkon-shki*
Wednesday	水曜日	*swee-yoh-bi*
week	週	*shoo*
weekend	週末	*shoo-mats*
weekly ticket	一週間の定期券	*isshookan-no tayki-ken*
welcome	いらっしゃい	*irassha-i*
well (good)	いい／良い	*ee/yoi*
well (water)	井戸	*ido*
west	西	*nishi*
wet	濡れた	*nureta*
wetsuit	ウェット・スーツ	*wetto-soots*
what?	何	*nani*
wheel	車輪	*sharin*
wheelchair	車いす	*kuruma-isu*
when?	いつ	*itsu*
where?	どこ	*doko*
which?	どちら	*dochira*
white	白い	*shiro-i*

who?	誰	daray
why?	なぜ	nazay
wide-angle lens	広角レンズ	kohkaku renzu
widow	未亡人	mibohjin
widower	男やもめ	otoko-yamomay
wife (other's)	奥さま	okusama
wife (own)	妻	tsuma
wi-fi	無線LAN／wi-fi	musen-ran/wai-fai
wi-fi built-in digital camera	Wi-fi 搭載デジカメ	wai-fai toh-sigh deji-kame
wind	風	kazay
windbreak	風よけ	kazay-yokay
windmill	風車	foosha
window	窓	mado
window (of ticket office)	窓口	mado-guchi
windshield wiper	ワイパー	wigh-pah
wine	ワイン	wign
wine list	ワインのメニュー	wign-no menyoo
wine shop	酒屋	saka-ya
winter	冬	fuyu
witness	証人	shoh-nin
woman	女	onna
wonderful (taste)	おいしい	oy-shee
wood	木	ki
wool (for knitting)	毛糸	kay-to
word	言葉	kotoba
work	仕事	shi-goto
worn	古くなった	furuku-natta
worried	心配な	shimpigh-na
wound	傷	kizu
wrap	包む	tsutsumu
wrist	手首	tekubi
write	書く	kaku
write down	書く	kaku
writing pad	便箋	binsen
writing paper	便箋	binsen
wrong	間違った	machi-gatta

Y

yacht	ヨット	yotto
year	年	toshi/nen
yellow	黄色い	kee-roy
yes	はい	high
yes, please	はい、いただきます／お願いします	high, itadaki-mas/ onegigh-shimas
yesterday	昨日	kinoh
yoga	ヨガ	yoga
yogurt	ヨーグルト	yohguruto
you	あなた	anata
you too	あなたも	anata-mo
youth hostel	ユースホステル	yoos-hosteru

Z

zip	ファスナー／ジッパー	fasunah/jippah
zoo	動物園	doh-butsu-en
zucchini	ズッキーニ	zukkeenee